If Nuns Ruled
the World

If Nuns Ruled the World

the World

Ten Sisters on a Mission

JO PIAZZA

OPEN ROAD

INTEGRATED MEDIA

NEW YORK

Cover design by Mauricio Díaz

978-1-4976-0190-1

Published in 2014 by Open Road Integrated Media, Inc.
345 Hudson Street
New York, NY 10014
www.openroadmedia.com

To Simone, Megan, Tesa, Nora, Dianna, Madonna, Donna, Joan, Maureen, and Jeannine. If nuns ruled the world, I have no doubt it would be a fairer place.

Contents

Author's Note

Strictly speaking, "women religious" refers to all women in the Church who have taken the vows of poverty, chastity, and obedience. By the strictest of definitions, "nuns" are a subset of women religious who are cloistered, contemplative, and dedicated to a life of prayer. "Sisters" are another subset, who pursue active work out in the world. However, these words have become so colloquially interchanged within and outside of the Church that we use them as synonyms here.

If Nuns Ruled the World

"Women think with their whole bodies and they see things as a whole more than men do."
—Dorothy Day

"Let us touch the dying, the poor, the lonely and the unwanted according to the graces we have received and let us not be ashamed or slow to do the humble work."
—Mother Teresa

Introduction

In December of 2013 the newly elected Pope Francis won out over NSA leaker Edward Snowden, gay-rights activist Edith Windsor, Syrian president Bashar al-Assad, and US president Barack Obama to be named *Time* magazine's "Person of the Year."

"He took the name of a humble saint and then called for a church of healing," *Time* wrote in its announcement about the decision. "The septuagenarian superstar is poised to transform a place that measures change by the century."

Ever since Jorge Mario Bergoglio, a Jesuit from Argentina, assumed the papacy in March of that same year, he was lauded as a potential reformer, praised for backing away from a focus on doctrine and moving toward a reinvigorated focus on service and compassion for the poor. And within a very short amount of time his actions began to help change the perception of the Church as out-of-touch.

"This focus on compassion, along with a general aura of merriment not always associated with princes of the church, has made Francis something of a rock star," wrote *Time* editor Nancy Gibbs.

He washed the feet of female convicts and opted to drive around in a used 1984 Renault. He chose to live in a Vatican hotel, rather than the fancy Apostolic palace. He eschews the security squadrons of the popes before him and takes "selfies" with his adoring fans.

The new pope was hailed as a progressive icon, and yet on the subject of women in the Church, he remained loyal to a long-held and antiquated stance: women cannot become priests.

"The reservation of the priesthood to males, as a sign of Christ the Spouse who gives himself in the Eucharist, is not a question open to discussion," he said in his first apostolic exhortation in November 2013. He insisted he wanted women and their "feminine genius" to contribute to the Church in other ways, just not as priests.

This book is about the feminine genius in the Catholic Church.

Catholic sisters and nuns rarely receive banner headlines or magazine covers. They eschew the spotlight by their very nature, and yet they're out there in the world every day, living the Gospel and caring for the poor. They don't hide behind fancy and expensive vestments, a pulpit, or a sermon. I have never met a nun who drives a Mercedes-Benz or a Cadillac. They walk a lot; they ride bikes.

Each woman profiled in this book deserves her own magazine cover. When we went to press, Sister Madonna Buder, at eighty-three years old, had competed in forty-six Ironman races. Sister Megan Rice, also eighty-three, was slated to spend the rest of her life in prison for staying strong in her beliefs that nuclear weapons need to be eliminated from the world. Sister Simone Campbell of NETWORK, a Catholic social justice lobby, drove across the country during the 2012 presidential election to stand up to vice presidential candidate Paul Ryan's social-service-slashing budget plan. Sister Joan Dawber was running a safe house for victims of human trafficking, and Sister Tesa Fitzgerald had just completed a $9 million luxury apartment building to provide affordable housing to female ex-felons and their children.

Writing in the *New York Times* in 2012, "Beliefs" columnist Mark Oppenheimer described the American attitude toward nuns as a "a safe nostalgia . . . [a] curiosity that we reserve for endangered species, like manatees, or Shakers."

Just as we were going to press with this book, the Internet exploded in a viral media frenzy over twenty-five-year-old Sister Cristina Scuccia. The Sicilian Ursuline sister appeared on the blind auditions for the Italian version of the reality television show *The Voice*, bopping around onstage in a full black habit to Alicia Keys's hit "No One," with perfect pitch and moves that rivaled Justin Bieber's. Within days the YouTube video of the audition received more than 19 million views. The world gushed over her. "For when you want a taste of sister act!" tweeted Whoopi Goldberg, the star of the movie *Sister Act*. The Vatican's minister of culture Gianfranco Ravasi also tweeted his admiration and even added a hashtag. "Each of you should use whatever gift you have received to serve others (1 Peter 4:10) #suorcristina."

No fewer than thirty-seven people sent me a link to Sister Cristina's video.

"Can you believe this?" they wrote. "A nun!" It was the same incredulous tone people use when they send you a video of the unlikely friendship between a dog and a wallaby or an astronaut singing David Bowie's "Space Oddity" while actually in space. The video of Sister Cristina getting down to Alicia Keys on television was such an oddity in itself that it jarred and excited people.

Three months later, Sister Cristina was crowned the winner of the Italian *Voice*, an honor that was accompanied by the promise of a recording contract with Universal Records. Learning of her win onstage, she gave the audience a thumps-up. Then she recited the Lord's Prayer.

"The last word of thanks, the most important, goes of

course to Him in heaven," she said. "And my dream is to recite a Padre Nostro together . . . I want Jesus to enter into this."

Her run on the show didn't pass without controversy. The more conservative Catholics castigated Cristina for wearing her habit onstage, while others brushed her off as a silly gimmick in a world of reality television shows desperate for ratings.

But Sister Cristina took to that stage and shattered stereotypes of Catholic nuns held by millions of people around the world. She did it in her way, and the nuns in these pages do it in theirs.

None of the women profiled in this book are content to remain in the annals of nostalgia. They are wise, they are wonderful, and they change the world every single day, not through grand edicts or declarations but through their actions, and living the way they believe Jesus would want them to live. The religion scholar, author, and former nun Karen Armstrong has described the roles of women in all of Christianity as limited to virgin, martyr, witch, wife, and mother. They don't often get to play the hero. I want to change that.

The first Catholic nun I encountered in the flesh was Sister Elaine Kuizinas, a Sister of St. Casimir and the principal of the Villa Joseph Marie High School for Girls in Holland, Pennsylvania. I was fourteen years old and simultaneously tugging on my frizzy, sun-bleached brown hair and the ends of a plaid kilt. I had been suspended from public school after a fight with a group of girls much scrappier and more experienced in fighting than I was. My parents hoped that Catholic girls' school might pray some sense into me. Sister Elaine stared a hole directly into my soul and admitted me on a trial basis. She made sure I knew I was a problem for her.

It was the 1990s, but still, black-and-white habits dotted the lush grounds of the school like lawn furniture. Most of the women were elderly and too frail to be standing in front of classrooms. Despite being surrounded by nuns, my view of them remained narrow and superficial.

I want to be clear from the start: I am not a religious person. I don't attend church on a regular basis, I use birth control, my best friend is a gay diplomat, and I have a problem being part of a Church that would tell the daughter I hope to have one day that there is something she cannot be: a priest. I am the product of an Italian American, lapsed-Catholic father who once tried to baptize me in an apple-bobbing tank at the Iowa State Fair, and a fair-weather Lutheran mother who once used a Bible as a doorstop.

Some scientists believe in the idea of a "God gene," a theory first posited by the geneticist Dean Hamer that explains there is a physiological basis for how spiritually connected a person feels to a higher power. Perhaps my lack of a God gene is what drew me to nuns in the first place. Perhaps I wanted to understand what exactly I was lacking. I was working on my master's thesis at New York University on how nuns use social media when I traveled down a rabbit hole and into the lives of women who shattered every stereotype I had about Catholic nuns during my high school years. The women I met were funny, inspiring, and fierce, and that was just in 140 characters or less. They were sassy. They reminded me of the sisters of Nonnberg Abbey in the film *The Sound of Music*, a movie I watched over and over with near religious fervor as a little girl. In one of my favorite scenes, Sister Margaretta and Sister Berthe approach the Reverend Mother to confess that they have sinned. They have torn distributor caps from the Nazis' cars in order to save the von Trapp family.

I may not believe in God, but I do believe in nuns.

I learned that nuns know when to laugh. The rest of us laugh because we feel obligated. Nuns reserve their laughter for things they genuinely find funny. They love puns. Tell a good "nunsense" joke and they're rolling. When they laugh, I promise you that you will laugh too.

I learned that nuns are truly excellent huggers—quick to embrace friends and even strangers, giving the good kind of hug, the kind that comes in strong, where their hands clasp around your middle so they embrace the back of your heart.

American nuns are under fire from the hierarchy of the Catholic Church, an institution whose stance on women can be described as bipolar at best. The Vatican has long grappled with how to keep nuns as loyal servants without affording them any of their own power.

The irony is that the very first Catholic nuns joined religious communities to gain more freedoms. In ancient times, women sought vocations with the young cult of Jesus Christ in search of a release from the patriarchal political system that subordinated them. By remaining celibate and serving God, the earliest nuns were considered apart from gender. They were referred to as "the virgins," considered neither male nor female, and as such, were able to escape being consigned to a life of procreation. But throughout history, the descendants of those virgins who sought freedom from men through religious life have become entrenched in a patriarchal system where their freedoms have been consistently infringed upon.

Suffice it to say, attacks on nuns are not exactly a modern phenomenon.

In the sixteenth century, the Council of Trent, a sweeping reaction to Protestant heresies during the start of the Reformation, handed down strict orders to protect the piety of religious women. Pope Pius V, the same pope who would excommunicate Queen Elizabeth I for daring to be born the illegitimate daughter of Henry VIII, penned the bull *Circa Pastoralis* on May 29, 1566, part of which was enacted specifically to protect a nun's virginity. The new legislation imprisoned the nuns by annexing them to cloisters where their purity would remain under lock and key. It decreed that nuns could not leave their convents or receive visitors unless approved by the bishop. To this end, there could be only one entrance to a convent so as to monitor arrivals and exits. Mothers Superior, the leaders of an order, conducted spot searches and destroyed any "contraband," including "books, clothes, writings, dishonest paintings, dogs, birds, or other animals." To allow for these searches, all personal locks were removed from the sisters' doors.

Today's nuns have not been held prisoner, but it is generally agreed in religious communities that the persecution from the patriarchy in the twenty-first century marks the greatest offense on nuns of the modern age. The most recent attacks began on December 22, 2008, when the Vatican's Congregation for Institutes of Consecrated Life and Societies of Apostolic Life, led by Cardinal Franc Rodé, a Slav priest from Buenos Aires, initiated an inquiry into the "quality of life" of nuns in America. This inquiry took on the formal title of "Apostolic Visitation," a euphemism for investigation. Previous "visitations" conducted by the Church were designed to probe Church officials who had gone astray. During the priest sexual abuse scandal, the Vatican ordered visitations of American seminaries. It also conducted a visitation of the Legionaries of Christ, a men's order whose founder, Fr. Marcial Maciel Degollado, abused young seminarians and fathered a child.

Nuns nicknamed the visitation process the "Great Nun-quisition." As I mentioned, they love puns. They viewed it as a by-product of the same increasingly conservative Vatican patriarchy that elected Joseph Aloisius Ratzinger to be pope in 2005 and was concerned about the progressive things nuns had been doing since shedding their habits in the 1960s—particularly some of their refusals to hold the Church party line on issues like abortion and gay rights.

The great irony is that it was the Vatican that *told* nuns they should shed their habits and live more independent lives in the first place. In 1962, Pope John XXIII launched a populist revolution in the Catholic Church with the Second Vatican Council. For the first time in more than a thousand years, Catholics could hear Mass in their native languages instead of Latin. Laypeople could take on leadership roles. The Church began to open up a dialogue with other religions, and nuns could take off their habits.

They were also given a newfound freedom.

Many sisters got their own apartments, drivers' licenses, and bank accounts. The Church expressly told them to "start looking at the signs of the times, look at where the people are suffering, look at where the people are in need," and it told the women to go to those places and find their callings there. This took the nuns out of schools and hospitals and placed them among the margins of society. Some women took up minority issues, including the rights of gays and lesbians. Some took on health-care issues; others fought for equal rights and women's rights. Some even began fighting for a woman's right to have an abortion.

Nuns knew charity wasn't enough. They wanted to be present in the lives of the poor. Inspired by the social movements of the 1960s and '70s to seek social justice through systemic change, many of them engaged in civil disobedience. Some even went to prison for their protests.

For the forty years between Vatican II and the millennium, nuns were largely left to their own devices. The recent Apostolic Visitation changed all that.

On paper, the probes were downplayed. The Church argued that they were looking out for the sisters' quality of life and just making sure they were adhering to Church doctrine. But the real purpose of the extensive investigation remained cloaked in secrecy. Many nuns did not know why they were being investigated at all.

Sister Maureen Fiedler, the host of the popular public radio talk show *Interfaith Voices*, was candid about the surprise that nuns felt when they discovered *they* were the ones under investigation. "These investigations came out of the clear blue sky, without any allegations of wrongdoing that usually prompt official probes," Fiedler said. "And they brought howls of protest from nuns themselves and many in the laity. Typical was the comment of a friend of mine: 'Now . . . let me get this straight. Some priests committed sex abuse. Bishops covered it up. And so they're investigating *nuns*?'"

Theories volleyed back and forth about the why of it. Did the Vatican want to put nuns back in habits and turn back the clock to pre–Vatican II? Did they want to go even further and put nuns back in cloisters à la the Council of Trent? One theory was that the Church was after the nuns' property. Still another maintained that the nuns had become a public relations crisis for the Church. Were the nuns so hip they made the rest of the Church look even more antiquated?

In the spring of 2010, the Visitation began on-site visits led by Mother Mary Clare Millea, a matronly American nun with a doctorate in canon law from Rome's Pontifical Lateran University. After visiting four hundred religious institutes across the country, Millea found herself unable to reproach the nuns. In her 2012 report to the Vatican she admitted that she had been humbled by their work.

"As I learned of and observed firsthand the perseverance of the religious in the United States in their vocations, in their ministries and in their faith—and witnessed the fruits of their service—I have been both inspired and humbled. Although there are concerns in religious life that warrant support and attention, the enduring reality is one of fidelity, joy, and hope," Millea said.

Nuns face another crisis outside of the Vatican—an aging population and a slowdown in recruitment. There has been more than a 70 percent decline in their numbers since 1965.

The number of Catholic nuns in America dropped from

179,954 in 1965 to 51,247 in 2013, according to George-town's Center for Applied Research in the Apostolate (CARA). Worldwide orders are not robust, but not in as dire straits as in the United States—globally the number of women religious dropped from 1,004,304 in 1970 to 721,935 in 2013.

Because of their dwindling numbers, Catholic nuns in America have been placed on a deathwatch. "American Catholics have no idea how very soon there will be no nuns," Sister Patricia Wittberg, a church sociologist at Indiana University, told the *Los Angeles Times* in 1994.

Sister Eleace King, a research associate at Georgetown's CARA, told me, "The majority of religious congregations of women in this country will not survive. Most are dying."

Nuns confuse people because they don't have many of the things Americans think of as the trappings of a good and "normal" life: marriage, kids, a sex life. The one thing everyone asks me when they find out I've been writing a book about nuns is: why would anyone choose that kind of life?

I asked the sisters that very question over and over again. I would be lying if I said I hadn't, at some point, wondered it myself.

The first part of nuns' answer to that question is spiritual. All of these women, at some point in their lives, but very often before puberty, felt a calling from God. Many describe the calling as an intense feeling that grew into a life-changing idea. This is practically unfathomable to someone lacking the God gene, but it is what I have heard consistently across almost each and every nun's personal narrative. I believe them.

The second part of the answer is practical. These women wanted to live an authentic life of service, and they couldn't do that as married women trying to raise a family. I also heard over and over again that nuns experience an uncommon sense of peace and happiness in their lives. We live in a society constantly searching for ways to live an authentic life. Nuns already do. They do exactly what they love, are unapologetic about it, and enjoy every single day to its fullest. There is a marked lack of regret, and an ability to live in the moment that is rare. They tell me that they don't feel like anything is missing. After conducting countless interviews with nuns, I can say that these women have no doubt that Jesus Christ is the great love of their lives and service is their highest calling.

The most interesting explanation I heard for the decision to eschew romantic relationships in favor of a symbolic marriage to Jesus came from a woman named Sara Marks. She is around my age, pretty and blond, with perfectly tousled curls and a penchant for mascara and funky earrings. She has a harmless addiction to buying beautiful scarves and loves a glass of white wine. When we met she was discerning—religious speak for training—to become a Franciscan sister in Aston, a Philadelphia suburb.

I told Marks I thought of her as a unicorn, since she is one of the incredibly rare women today seeking to become a nun in her twenties. I found her through her blog titled "Mascara and Prayer," and we soon started talking about how she reconciled giving up the fairy tale of a wedding, husband, and kids. Marks was so matter-of-fact that I was taken aback.

"I wanted the first five years. I wanted the engagement, the wedding, having the baby, and I never thought beyond that—about living the day-to-day with one person for the rest of my life. Once I thought beyond it, I was able to give it up. I realized I was more in love with the *idea* of those things than the reality of them."

Marks said no to being a nun for about seven years, but she kept dipping her toes in and out of the vocation. She'd be on a date on a Friday and on a retreat with the sisters on Saturday.

"How do you tell somebody you're dating that you're considering becoming a nun?" I asked her.

"You don't," she said. "It's like living a double life."

One of the final signs she was ready to become a sister came when she read her journal. She realized that every time she wrote about being sad or lonely, it had to do with a man. When she wrote about feeling happy and fulfilled, it was when she was spending time in a community of sisters. She professed her first vows as a Sister of St. Francis on the Feast of St. Clare in August of 2013.

That sense of emotional fulfillment is mostly universal across the sisters I spoke with. This emotional stability and sense of peace makes nuns a real joy to be around. Like their laughter, it is contagious.

God has become a character in these chapters. It is an occupational hazard when writing about the lives of nuns. In these pages, God means a lot of different things: a friend, protector, confidante. Sometimes God is just the hand of the universe shuffling the deck of our lives.

While most of the stories I have worked on in my career as a journalist seem completely unrelated to one another, I believe there is a common thread. What I most enjoy doing is treating the extraordinary stories of ordinary people the way most of our media today treats the lives of celebrities. Have you ever noticed that everything a celebrity does is inherently fascinating to us? They walk down the street, they get a coffee, have a wardrobe malfunction, take their kids to the playground, fight with their spouse, or adopt a puppy, and it could be the most-read news of the day.

I need to admit right here and now that this is partially my fault. I have worked in the entertainment sections of newspapers, magazines, and television news networks for years. That makes me feel a bit guilty. Some might call that Catholic guilt. Perhaps that is why I want to tell the stories of these nuns as if they were rock stars or Hollywood royalty. My guilt aside, this is exactly the kind of platform they deserve, more so than any starlet I have covered.

I wanted to write a book that showed nuns as people as opposed to stereotypes.

The women in these pages have done extraordinary things.

Each of them has changed her corner of the world for the better. The fact that they have accomplished so much while yoked to an institution that actively and publicly sets out to quash their activities makes what they have done that much more remarkable.

I originally titled this book *Bad Habit: The Secret Lives of Nuns*. I, too, like a good pun. But the thing is, none of these women is a secret. They don't do their good works behind closed doors. They aren't trying to pull the wool over anyone's eyes. They are out in the open, making the world a better place.

1.

Weapons Are Made Like Gods

Putting trust in weapons is idolatry. Weapons are always false gods because they make money. It's profiteering.

—Sister Megan Rice

She couldn't keep walking. Sister Megan Rice had been training for this moment for months, but she was tired and kept slipping to her knees into the prickled shrubs and the high grass as she willed herself up the hill to the Y-12 National Security Complex in Oak Ridge, Tennessee.

The eighty-two-year-old nun was the mastermind of this plan—a plan that, once completed, would become known as the biggest security breach in the history of the nation's atomic complex. But she was also the weak link. A person half her age would have been exhausted as they scaled the steep and densely wooded hill on the path into the heart of Y-12.

It was the very early morning of July 28, 2012, when Megan, a vowed Sister of the Society of the Holy Child Jesus, and two accomplices—Gregory I. Boertje-Obed, age fifty-seven, and Michael R. Walli, age sixty-three, both US veterans—broke into the nuclear weapons facility. Using bolt cutters, the three of them first infiltrated an exterior boundary fence, six feet high with bright-yellow No Trespassing placards threatening a $100,000 fine and up to one year in prison. Sister Megan went first. The men mended the fence behind her with twine, and together they began the forty-degree ascent.

The plan was to hike along the ridge of the hill, breach another set of fences, and then walk toward the facility, which houses the nation's cache of highly enriched uranium—enough to fuel more than 10,000 nuclear bombs.

"Megan has trouble going up hills, so we walked at an angle," Mr. Boertje-Obed told me. "We just kept going to the right. Megan was so tired when we got to the top that I said, 'Let's just go to the first building that we happen to see.'" Next they negotiated through an infrared intrusion detection system called the PIDAS, a perimeter intrusion detection and assessment system.

"The motion detectors are set off often by wildlife," Ralph

Hutchinson, a friend of the three, a co-conspirator, and the coordinator for the Oak Ridge Environmental Peace Alliance told me. "That's why they were ignored. One of the cameras that would have picked them up was malfunctioning, and the other camera did pick them up but the guard wasn't looking at it."

The one thing they all agreed on was that they felt they were being led by the Almighty.

Maybe they were. Some kind of providence was with them that night. The first building they happened upon was the big one, the site's mother lode for nuclear storage—a billion-dollar Highly Enriched Uranium Materials Facility. That was where they would carry out their mission.

Y-12 in Oak Ridge, Tennessee, was where the nuclear age began. Ground was broken on February 18, 1943, in the midst of World War II, for an electromagnetic separation plant—or, in layman's terms, a place that could make enough enriched uranium for a new kind of bomb. The atom bomb. At peak production in 1945, more than 22,000 workers were producing enriched uranium for Little Boy, the bomb the *Enola Gay* dropped on Hiroshima that killed approximately 60,000 civilians and ultimately ended World War II in the Pacific. During the Cold War, more than 8,000 people worked at Y-12 to make nuclear weapon "secondaries"—the components of a nuclear weapon's secondary explosive that are compressed by nuclear fission from the primary explosive and generate the crux of explosive energy.

Once inside the facility, Sister Megan and her co-conspirators swung banners over the walls: WOE TO AN EMPIRE OF BLOOD, one declared. They looped panicked yellow crime-scene tape reading NUCLEAR CRIME SCENE around the site. They chipped bits of concrete from the wall with small hammers.

"Just a little. It wasn't violent," Sister Megan told me as she remembered mustering her strength to bang on the wall. "Violence was not an option." She was adamant that the protest not be violent. "Even if we were attacked by dogs after we broke in, I would have just raised my hands," she said. "I would have let the dogs take me down."

Leading up to the break-in the trio had held conversations about whether they would be shot by guards. That was a risk they were willing to take.

They had brought with them six baby bottles filled with human blood (siphoned from three living humans supportive of their cause) and poured them onto the building before conducting a liturgical ceremony with white roses, lit candles, and the breaking of bread. They had chosen Sunday for their break-in as much for its spiritual significance as for the fact that they believed there would be fewer guards on patrol. When a guard finally reached the three trespassers at 4:30 a.m., they did not flinch and instead tendered some of their bread to him as an offering.

That guard, Kirk Garland, a sturdy man with a broad face weathered by the lines of Southern living, was authorized to use deadly force, but at first it all appeared so innocent. All Garland saw was an old woman and a couple of unshaven men. Maybe they were just a painting crew. Then he saw the messages spray-painted on the wall behind them. He read the words and when it clicked that these were intruders he called for backup. Five minutes later a second security guard appeared, this one brandishing an M16 weapon. Sister Megan sang "This Little Light of Mine" as she was placed in handcuffs. The last time that she looked at her watch, it was a quarter to five in the morning.

"They were passive," Mr. Garland would later say during his testimony against them after he lost his $85,000-a-year job, just four years from retirement. Sister Megan would later express remorse at her involvement in Mr. Garland's dismissal, saying she hoped he would find another job in security, preferably somewhere less destructive. "Like a bank," she said.

For the Y-12 break-in, Sister Megan, Mr. Boertje-Obed, and Mr. Walli were charged with destruction and depredation of government property, both felonies. The intrusion caused $8,531.67 in physical damages, according to Y-12 officials. It took 100 gallons of paint to cover up the spray-painted graffiti and human blood and to repair the fences. The security breach also damaged Y-12's credibility as a safe haven for special nuclear materials. If a little old nun and a couple of out-of-shape middle-aged men could get that close to the heart of the complex, what was stopping the terrorists?

"All three of them were elated that they were able to do so much," said Ellen Barfield, a fellow peace activist and the one phone call Sister Megan made from jail after the arrest. With a flick of her hand, Barfield added, with none of the gravitas the statement should have required, "Plus, they were mildly pleased that they were still alive."

Frank Munger, the *Knoxville News Sentinel* senior reporter who covers the paper's Department of Energy issues, has been on the Y-12 beat for three decades. He told me that in the aftermath of the July arrest, plenty of residents of Knoxville thought that the guards should not have hesitated.

"You heard people say they should have shot them," Mr. Munger said nonchalantly during my visit to the offices of the *Sentinel*. Sister Megan really likes Frank Munger. He became her de facto biographer after she was arrested, and she talks about him like a proud mother, bragging about how thorough he was in his reporting of Y-12, even when it painted her in a less than pleasant light.

"He is a very special person," she confided. "Special" is a vote of confidence from Sister Megan. Even though she is incapable of insulting anyone, when she doesn't respect a person, she chooses not to answer questions about them at all. She just clams up and minutes later will change the subject.

Y-12 is the largest employer in this small section of Tennessee, with more than 9,000 workers in the area. Residents hate it when other people, especially Northerners, come to town and cause a scene. "In East Tennessee, the worst sin is to draw attention to yourself," Ralph Hutchinson told me. "The second worst is to break rules. These people don't break rules here."

Oak Ridge is an insular place, situated between the jagged bends of the Clinch River and five Appalachian ridges and valleys. Just twenty-five miles west of Knoxville, folks in Oak Ridge don't take to outsiders. It's a town that once detained Santa Claus because they didn't like the cut of his beard. There is a famous picture of Jolly Old Saint Nick from 1948, one hand in the air, a toy in the other, being detained and searched by two armed guards as he attempted to get into the first annual Oak Ridge National Laboratory Christmas party.

I traveled down to Eastern Tennessee at Sister Megan's invitation, just days before Thanksgiving in 2012, hoping to meet with her and her legal team as they prepared for a pretrial hearing for the Y-12 break-in.

"We can drive back together and you can stay with me," Sister Megan told me in her soft and measured voice that rarely rises above a whisper, over the phone from Rosemont, Philadelphia, where she lived with her order.

When an eighty-two-year-old nun facing federal prison for the rest of her life asks you to go on a road trip with her, you don't hesitate. I had been covering the presidential election for nine months straight, and I thought a good old Southern trial might be the perfect antidote to my political languor.

"There's this nun down in Knoxville facing life in prison," I said to my boss, Victor Balta, the managing editor of the website for Current TV. He was skeptical.

"She is a peace activist, broke into a nuclear weapons facility," I explained breathlessly. Then, for good measure: "Nuclear disarmament is a big issue with our viewers. Plus . . . she's eighty-two." Victor gave me the two days off as long as I paid for my own plane ticket.

I booked a one-way ticket to Knoxville and flew two legs coach early on a Monday morning, the second of which was filled with sweaty and statuesque members of the University of Tennessee men's basketball team. Sister Megan, who doesn't drive, arranged for a member of the Oak Ridge Environmental Peace Alliance (OREPA) to greet me at the airport. Carol, a United Methodist in her sixties, was wearing a flower-patterned embroidered vest when she met me en route to baggage claim carrying a sign written in black marker that read NAMASTE. Carol filled me in on the history of Y-12, to which she referred as both the nation's "nuclear insecurity complex" and the "bomb plant," always with a girlish giggle, as we drove along the highway past the kinds of motels that advertise $199 for a one-week stay.

Our destination was the basement of St. John's Cathedral in downtown Knoxville, where Sister Megan was meeting with her legal team in advance of the hearing. It was the first time we met in person, but Sister Megan greeted me with a hug like we were old friends.

The temperature was a moderate fifty-five degrees in Knoxville that day, but Sister Megan looked ready for a family ski trip in a soft gray wool sweater, lavender hoodie, fleece vest, and navy sweatpants. "I'm always too cold," she said with a small shiver. I could feel her shoulder blades through four layers of clothing. She grabbed my rough hand in her small soft one and we walked down the dimly lit hall together. It is hard to describe what Sister Megan's presence is like. She projects an aura of calm that washes over everyone near her. Three coffees and an early morning flight had made me jumpy, but she made me feel at ease. There is a force and a vitality that transcends her tiny body.

Sitting in the basement's spacious conference room were OREPA's Ralph Hutchinson, a crunchy Richard Dreyfuss doppelgänger, and Kary Love, an advising counsel partial to black turtlenecks and cowboy boots, who had driven down from Michigan for the hearing. Compared to Hutchinson in his slightly ripped jeans, beard, and hiking sneakers, Mr. Love, who had been trying nuclear disarmament cases for the better part of three decades, looked the part of the dashing antagonist in a daytime soap opera.

"I long ago recognized that were Jesus to return, many of those imprisoned in US federal prisons today for peaceful demonstrations against US nuke weapons would be those with whom he would associate. Megan Rice, I believe, is one of those," Mr. Love told me.

Standing, huddled in a corner, were Francis Lloyd, the local Knoxville attorney, and Bill Quigley, a dapper law professor from Loyola University New Orleans.

Thousands of civil disobedience cases are tried each year, and while the group gathered in the basement was keen to focus on the grander issues surrounding nuclear disarmament, they couldn't ignore the fact that they were sitting on public relations gold with this particular case.

"What they're asking for is the death penalty for an octogenarian nun," Mr. Love declared, his voice rising in excitement and his fist rapping on the distinguished dark wood table in the church basement conference room. He wanted no less than to start a petition asking that Sister Megan receive the Presidential Medal of Freedom rather than sixteen years in prison. "Hopefully because of the buzz with Sister Rice, we get enough media attention that people all over the world sign up," Mr. Love said.

Everyone in the room agreed that the more awareness they could bring to "the nun thing," the better off their case would be.

"If you guys were willing to cross-dress, we'd get more attention," Mr. Hutchinson said to Sister Megan's male co-conspirators. "It would be the cute little nun and the not-so-cute other nuns."

Sister Megan stayed quiet and wrapped a fleece blanket around her shoulders, even though the basement was a little bit warm. She was the only one reluctant to play the nun card. "It's not about me. It's about the three of us, and the message," she quietly told me.

The nun card was a thing that commanded attention, though, attracting reporters from the Associated Press, the *New York Times,* and the *Washington Post* for a story that wouldn't have otherwise gotten much attention outside of the Blue Ridge Mountains. Dan Zak, a reporter for the *Post* who wrote a pitch-perfect account of the break-in, aftermath, and trial, described it to me as perfect casting for the perfect news story.

"A break-in at Y-12 would have made a splash because of Megan's age, but you add on top of that the fact that she is a nun, and people really perk up," Zak told me. "First off you did have this older woman doing this thing, but then she was also a nun, doing something that most people wouldn't consider nunlike at all."

It was strangely warm for November, even in the South, and from St. John's it was just a meandering five-minute walk across the red and gold tree-lined Cumberland Avenue to the Howard H. Baker Jr. Courthouse in Knoxville's town center. Sister Megan was happy for the little bit of exercise. "I have to get it in while I can," she joked, the first of many I'm-probably-going-to-prison-soon cracks she made during our time together. The Baker courthouse is something straight out of a Hollywood movie—pristine, white, and unapologetically antebellum in design. Until the mid-1930s it was home to the publishing empire of a gentleman named Chris Whittle. The four-block campus, with its 250,000-square-foot neo-Georgian building, was once the headquarters for Whittle's nine hundred employees and hub for forty media products, including nineteen magazines and the youth news program Channel One, most famous for giving CNN stalwart Anderson Cooper his first newsanchor job. When Whittle's empire unraveled and the scraps of the company moved in a reverse carpetbag to New York City, the elaborate campus was sold off to the federal government.

Sister Megan threw her shoulders back as she strode through the pristine white doors of the courthouse and past a statue of Lady Justice. Scarred by bird feces and wearing an odd Indian headdress, the mistress of the law faces away from the entrance to the Knoxville federal court.

No one told the nun where she should sit, so she found a practical place in the third row of the courtroom. "When you're the guest of honor, you get to sit up front," her attorney, Mr. Lloyd, told her. She hugged him in thanks and he guided her to the defendant's table by her elbow. Nearly dwarfed by the great piece of furniture, she sat calmly and quietly, placing her two index fingers in a steeple supporting her chin.

The section for the audience was split into two sides like at a formal wedding, the defense on the right and the prosecution on the left. The right side was filled with gray-haired peace activists who held hands and sang "Peace Is Flowing Like a River" before the start of the proceedings. The prosecution, conservative in their well-tailored suits, glanced sideways at them with thinly masked disdain.

"The defendants know a lot of people think they're fools," Bill Quigley told me when he noted my own sideways glance during the hand-holding and the folk singing. "They know the judge and the prosecutors are looking down on them, but they don't care. They're totally at peace with themselves and what they are doing."

That day, the defense team argued to dismiss the charges against their clients on the basis of the presumed illegality of nuclear weapons under international law. The prosecution, meanwhile, was just keen to keep any conversation of morality and religion out of their courtroom. They knew the defense would play up the fact that Sister Megan was a nun and they wanted to neutralize it from the start.

"The whole legal process is trying to muzzle them so they can't explain what happened. They will be gagged in court and stripped of any meaningful way to have a defense," Mr. Quigley told me. "The chances of them being convicted will be extremely high . . . even Sister Megan. They want to seem tough enough to justify themselves to other people. Nobody wants to be the one who sentences a nun to die in prison."

Sister Megan is resilient, but she is not invincible. Just

two months prior to her hearing in Knoxville for the Y-12 incident, she shattered both wrists after tripping over a box in the Washington, DC, office of the group Witness for Peace and had to have surgery on both joints. She circled them, first in one direction, then in the other, as the attorneys argued over what kinds of evidence would be allowed into the courtroom. Their arguments went on for hours, leading nowhere. It would be weeks before Judge C. Clifford Shirley would make any kind of decision, months before it went to trial, and almost a year before a jury would reach a verdict.

I had planned on staying in a hotel that night, one of the Days Inns littered along the highway, but Sister Megan wouldn't hear of it. She insisted that I come to a dinner with the group and then stay with one of the peace activists. "You're one of us now," she said, clapping me on the back before offering up half her own bed at the home of a woman named Shelly. "I don't think I snore," she told me. "And I don't take up very much room at all."

For dinner we visited a restaurant called King Tut's for what was promised to be the best Middle Eastern food in all of Knoxville. Their specialty was a Greek salad the size of a watermelon.

"We take all of our criminals here," Ralph Hutchinson joked as he passed me some couscous.

I immersed myself in the OREPA community that night, driving for a late-night dumpster dive to retrieve a Thanksgiving meal from the bins behind Trader Joe's and sleeping on the couch of Ralph's ex-wife, Lisa, kept warm by three eight-week-old kittens nestled on my belly.

Dawn hadn't yet broken when we prepared to start the journey home. Sister Megan asked that we say the Prayer for the Traveler before we began the 487-mile road trip. We clasped hands and I moved my mouth along to words I had never heard:

> *O Almighty and merciful God, who hast commissioned Thy angels to guide and protect us, command them to be our assiduous companions from our setting out until our return; to clothe us with their invisible protection; to keep from us all danger of collision, of fire, of explosion, of fall and bruises, and finally, having preserved us from all evil, and especially from sin, to guide us to our heavenly home. Through Jesus Christ our Lord, Amen.*

Sister Megan knows how to pack lightly, and she'd brought one outfit with many layers for the four-day trip. For our car ride, she wore the same sweater and lavender hoodie from the day before, topped off with a bright-red woolen cap and gray poncho, as she offered to sit in the middle of the backseat of the rented PT Cruiser. "You take the window, sweetie. You'll want to look at the scenery," she said to me through a brief cough. Sister Megan was en route to DC to spend the weekend at the Dorothy Day Worker House, while I would be in the city to say good-bye to my best friend, Matt, a Foreign Service Officer about to ship off to China for two years. As we drove through the suburban neighborhoods on the outskirts of Knoxville, Sister Megan asked me dozens of questions about what my friend would be doing in China. She told me she would pray for him.

"I've been lucky that I have been able to travel the world," she told me, raising her eyebrows above the silver rim of her lightly tinted oval glasses with the energy that comes only from the anticipation of a story about to be told.

Born on January 31, 1930, the nuclear nun, as the newspapers would eventually call her, spent her first few years in Connecticut before her family moved to a wealthy block on Claremont Avenue in the Morningside Heights neighborhood of New York City. She was the youngest of three girls, two of whom would become Catholic sisters. Her mother used to joke that she was becoming a nursery for the Holy Child order. Her father was an obstetrician who taught at New York University and treated patients at Bellevue Hospital. Her mother had gone to college at Barnard with the anthropologist Margaret Mead, got a master's from Columbia in history, and then received her doctorate there. She wrote her dissertation on Catholic views about slavery, one of the first studies that could rightly be called African American history. Good Upper West Side liberals, her parents were both heavily involved in the Catholic Worker movement from its early days and were close friends with its founder, Dorothy Day. Sister Megan remembers copies of the *Catholic Worker* newspaper scattered around her house like bits of carpet. It was on its pages that she first learned about concepts like pacifism and voluntary poverty, ideas that rattled about in her young brain and made her acutely aware of the extreme poverty and unspeakable suffering taking place right outside her door.

As a Depression baby, she said, "I had a desire to try to make the world a more fair place." The conversations around her at the dinner table centered on how to transform the lack of fairness and justice in the world, how to eliminate discrimination.

At fifteen, Megan was away at a summer camp in Maine run by the Diocese of Portland when the first nuclear bomb was dropped on Hiroshima.

"They told us this terrible bomb had been exploded," Sister Megan told me, recalling that her mother learned of the bombing from reading the *New York Daily News* as she emerged from the 116th Street subway station in Manhattan. "Atom Bomb Dropped on Japan," the headline read.

"I had an ominous feeling that it was awful and horrible," Sister Megan said.

By then she knew that she wanted to be a nun, mainly because she wanted to be of service to the world. At the

JO PIAZZA

time, in the 1940s, her options were limited. There was no Peace Corps yet, no NGO she could work for.

At St. Walburga's Academy on 140th Street and Riverside Drive, Megan was taught by a woman by the name of Sister Mary Laurentina Dalton, one of the pioneering nuns who had volunteered to teach children in Nigeria at the time. Sister Mary was the Latin teacher but injected tales of her time in Nigeria into nearly every lesson.

"By the time I was a senior, I really wanted to get there as quickly as I could and get to Africa," Sister Megan said about joining Sister Mary's order, the Society of the Holy Child Jesus, at age eighteen. "They were sending sisters to help begin the education of women in West Africa and so I was very much attracted to that, especially because of the incidents of discrimination. Teachers were needed there more than they were needed in the United States, and I thought perhaps I could fill that gap."

But first Megan received a bachelor's degree in secondary school biology from Villanova University and then a master's from Boston College. Once in Africa, her first station was very rural, in an area where they had never had a school, let alone a school for girls. Megan and her fellow sisters opened the first school for girls in 1962. With no housing for miles, at night they slept in the classroom without electricity or running water.

She continued her work as a science teacher in Nigeria on and off for the next twenty years. During a civil war in

40

1963, Sister Megan was briefly evacuated to Cameroon. To flee the country, she perched on top of a boat with twelve other sisters wearing their full formal habits, long skirts flapping in the breeze as they rode the swell of the waves amidst the treble of gunfire.

In the 1970s, Sister Megan was given the opportunity to study scripture in Sinai.

"In Palestine we walked two miles every day up and down the Mount of Olives. It was quite an up-and-down, let me tell you," she said, remembering the acropolis of the ancient Judean kingdom and the place where Jesus is believed to have ascended to heaven. She also did pastoral studies in Kenya, where she integrated Bible study with courses on justice, death, and dying.

Everything changed when she returned to Manhattan in the 1980s and started attending anti-nuclear protests. Living at the Catholic Worker house in Harlem, near her mother, who was by then living on her own after the passing of her father, Sister Megan found a home in the activist movement. When she was feeling up to it, her mother would accompany her to anti-nuclear protests. In 1998, Sister Megan was arrested for the first time while protesting at the School of the Americas, an Army school at Fort Benning, Georgia, where generations of Latin American soldiers were taught to fight leftist insurgencies. She was sentenced to six months in prison. Sister Megan arrived at the Muskogee County Jail in Oklahoma at five in the evening. The prisoners were ready for her after seeing a local news segment about a nun arriving at their facility. They were so excited to be made a little bit famous. A group came and hugged her when she walked in.

As Sister Megan told it, sixty-four women lived there in a facility built for thirty-two. "The excess women slept on mats on the floor. They just gave you a mat and a blanket and a sheet and a few little things. I was put in a pod with two women. One was a larger woman, so there was no thought of her getting off the bottom bunk. The other woman got off of the top bunk for me and moved underneath the bed with her mat," she told me with tears in her eyes. "You just cannot imagine the goodness of those women."

Our route out to Washington took us through the dark green Appalachian foothills, parallel to the border of West Virginia, through nameless old coal-mining towns. We stopped at a Waffle House outside of Roanoke and without asking me, Sister Megan spooned a heaping bite of greasy home fries doused in salt, pepper, and ketchup into my mouth like I was an infant. "You've been working so hard, you need food," she said like the kindly grandmother I never had.

As we continued the drive, she alternated between the past and the future, reading her Bible—a well-worn book covered in hand-carved leather from a student she once taught in Nigeria—and pecking away at her iPad, a gift from a friend. She called it her "toy."

My patience was tested five hours into the trip. Mr. Boertje-Obed slept in the passenger seat for most of the journey. Mr. Walli was partial to long and drawn-out diatribes on everything from the plethora of uneaten food thrown away each year in our country and the completely intact human skeleton he once found in a trash can, to drone warfare and conspiracy theories about 9/11. I felt bad asking him to be quiet for a while so that I could hear Sister Megan talk, but he didn't listen to me anyway. Sister Megan was able to silence him just by saying his name.

"Michael." She dropped her voice on the second syllable, and for the first time since I met him, Mike Walli stopped speaking and shifted his gaze out the window.

Sister Megan was struggling, trying to pull up a news article for me about the priest Roy Bourgeois, a friend and activist priest who was dismissed from his Maryknoll order and excommunicated for his belief that women should be allowed to become Catholic priests. After five minutes of error pages, I reached over her and tapped a few terms into Google to find what she needed, making the article appear in seconds. The corners of Sister Megan's tiny mouth curled up and she grabbed my hand. "So impressive," she said. "You will have to teach me how to be better at using this." Something in me softened. "I will." I smiled. Months later I would mail her a new iPad case with a keyboard attached that would make it easier for her to type through the pain in her wrists. That is part of what makes Sister Megan so special. You feel good about helping her and want to multiply that feeling of goodness in the world.

"Are you afraid of being excommunicated like Roy Bourgeois?" I asked her.

She yawned as if it were a silly question. "I don't believe in excommunication, because I don't see the institutional Church as the real Church."

She napped for about an hour after that, her breathing growing shallow as she gently snored on my shoulder. When she woke up, I was anxious to get in as many questions as possible in the remaining hour that we had together. I asked her if she was scared of prison.

She thought for a moment, curling her lower lip under the top in a way that made her resemble a wise tortoise. "No," she told me.

"If I go, I would like to go to Alderson. I've never been there," she said, tucking her hands, one with a gold band signifying her marriage to Jesus Christ and the other with a matching black band representing her solidarity with the poor, into her fleece vest. She said it in the tone that other older women might use to remark that they haven't gotten to see the Broadway show *Jersey Boys* yet.

Alderson is the all-women's federal prison in the Allegheny foothills of West Virginia. The women's facility gained attention in 2005 when lifestyle acolyte Martha Stewart famously knitted a poncho there during her five-month stay.

44

"If I go in, I will observe the goodness of the women. I could minister to the women and them to me," she said.

I asked her if she had any regrets about what she had done to the Y-12 facility and she gave her head a small shake. I tried another question. "Any regrets in general? About your life?"

She sighed. "I just wish I had done something about nuclear weapons earlier," she said. "I've known about this since I was nine years old, but it took me so long to finally do something."

In 2005, the Society of the Holy Child Jesus gave Sister Megan permission to join the Nevada Desert Experience, an activist group based in Las Vegas that organizes spiritual events near atomic test sites in support of nuclear abolition. Still, she wanted to take things further than a small protest here and there.

She was inspired to break into Y-12 by the work of another nun named Anne Montgomery. In November 2009, two Catholic priests and Montgomery, then eighty-one years old, along with two grandmothers unaffiliated with the Catholic Church, cut their way through two fences of a US naval base near Seattle and smeared the base with fake blood to protest nuclear weapons. That base was a home port for eight of the nation's fourteen Trident nuclear submarines and reportedly had one of the largest stockpiles of nuclear warheads in the country. The five successfully cut through three chain-link fences and penetrated a "shoot to kill" zone where nuclear weapons were said to be stored in concrete bunkers. They were apprehended and detained by Marines, and later, a jury convicted them on a range of crimes, including conspiracy to trespass. A US Court of Appeals for the Ninth Circuit upheld their convictions, and Montgomery served more than three years in prison.

Sister Anne was sent home with an ankle-monitoring bracelet that kept her on a tight leash, but Sister Megan was allowed to drive her to Mass every Saturday night.

How can I get involved? Sister Megan had asked Sister Anne during one of their drives.

"Call Greg Boertje-Obed," Sister Anne told her.

Mr. Boertje-Obed was a Presbyterian Iowa farm boy who had joined the ROTC so that he could afford Tulane University before going into active duty at Fort Polk in 1981 in the midst of the Cold War. He left the Army as a conscientious objector and returned to New Orleans, where he found a home in nuclear disarmament activism. While living in Jonah House, a Catholic Worker residence in Baltimore, he met his wife, Michele, and had a daughter. They scheduled their protests against an array of weapons facilities to ensure only one of them would be in jail at any given time so that someone was able to raise her.

Twenty-six years later, Sister Megan called him. After nearly six months of contemplation she set her sights on the facility in Oak Ridge, and together, they began planning their Y-12 action in late 2011.

"It was very organic. It was responding to the needs of the times," Sister Megan said. "I knew that my health was good. The moment was urgent." All of the information on Y-12's layout was available online. It was more than enough for them to make a map and plan how they would break into the facility. It was easier than they thought it would be—until they were caught by Kirk Garland.

We arrived safely in Washington, DC, and then kept in touch through e-mail and phone calls for the next nine months. It was nearly a year from that first hearing I attended in Knoxville that a verdict was finally passed down.

After just under two and a half hours of deliberation on May 8, 2013, a federal jury of nine men and three women found the protestors guilty of injuring the national defense and damaging government property during their break-in, a conviction with a maximum prison sentence of thirty years.

The two US attorneys argued that the defendants targeted and intruded upon the facility in Oak Ridge to disrupt its operations and that such a disruption imperiled national security.

"When you interfere with Y-12, you are interfering with the national defense," Jeff Theodore, the assistant US attorney for the case, told jurors in his closing arguments. The defense argued their clients never expected to make it as far as they did and that their goal was to promote the cause of disarmament through symbolic action.

Sister Megan smiled peacefully as the bailiff read the verdict.

"Guilty on all counts."

She flipped her palms open and raised her eyes up to the Lord. Dan Zak from the *Washington Post* was in the audience and couldn't take his eyes off of her. He described the moment perfectly to me: "She was just this beacon of acceptance and love even though this heavy judgment had just been levied against her. She was so completely Christ-like right then."

Her supporters sang softly: *"Love, love, love, love. People, we are made for love."* Sister Megan blew them a kiss as she was whisked away.

Seven months later, Sister Megan sat in prison awaiting sentencing. She spent Christmas that year in the Irwin County Detention Center in Ocilla, Georgia. In February she was handed a thirty-five-month jail term. She was content. Her lawyer, Bill Quigley, promised me that she was in "terrific spirits and really good health."

Her only complaint, as always, was that the prison wasn't warm enough. To keep the cold at bay she wore two jump-suits and long underwear, and wrapped a blanket around herself. According to Mr. Quigley, she never has a down moment. "For Megan this is a win-win situation. She always thinks it is a blessing to be exactly where she is."

2.

The Nun on the Bus

We're faithful to the Gospel. We work every day to live as Jesus did in relationship to the people in the margins of society. That's all we do.

—Sister Simone Campbell

Now, Sister, you and your fellow nuns have clearly gone rogue. You're radical feminists," the comedian Stephen Colbert said with a straight face as he reprimanded Sister Simone Campbell on his Comedy Central television show.

It was a hot June afternoon in the summer of 2012, and Mr. Colbert was shaking his head, even though a hint of a smile danced at the ends of his lips.

Sister Simone, dressed in a white blazer over a turquoise blouse, a jazzy patterned skirt, and a simple strand of pearls replied with a sly grin: "We're certainly oriented towards the needs of women, and responding to their needs. If that's radical, I guess we are."

"Yes, yes, that's *radical feminism*," Mr. Colbert retorted.

Just a few days later, the conservative radio host Rush Limbaugh, with none of the satire, took a more mean-spirited jab at her and her "posse" of radical sisters.

"You know what the nuns are doing? The nuns have gone feminazi on everyone," Limbaugh said. To put that comment in perspective, the right-wing host's comparison of the Catholic sisters to the Third Reich came just months after Limbaugh called Georgetown University Law student Sandra Fluke a "slut" and a "prostitute" when she testified in front of the House of Representatives on the importance of requiring insurance plans to cover contraception for all women.

If you don't know who Sister Simone is, then you are probably wondering what she had possibly done to command all of this attention. In the spring of 2012, Sister Simone was the mastermind of a brilliant rebranding of what it meant to be a nun in the twentieth century. She organized NETWORK's Nuns on the Bus, an epic road trip across America protesting the Republican "Path to Prosperity" budget plan proposed by congressman and vice presidential candidate Paul Ryan, that sought to slash the national deficit by $4.4 trillion by cutting funding for food stamps, social services, and other things desperately needed by the poor.

That tour turned Sister Simone and a handful of Catholic sisters, most well into their sixties and seventies, into media rock stars.

In the months that followed, Sister Simone appeared on every major news network in the country and on dozens of radio programs. They loved her at Comedy Central. While she was doing a segment with *Daily Show* correspondent Samantha Bee, the comedian jokingly asked her if she got a new car every year like the priests did. Sister Simone replied honestly that her order was poor, so she rode her clunky Schwinn everywhere. After the segment, Sister Simone admitted to the producers that one of her sins was bike envy. She had once ridden her brother's new lightweight Trek mountain bike and had fallen in love with it. A few weeks later she got a handwritten note from Ms. Bee and her producer, Miles, thanking her for being a guest and a good sport. They also let her know they had called her brother, asked for the model number of his bike, and purchased her an exact copy. All she had to do was pick it up.

"It's like heaven," she told me when I admired the bike while we were having coffee in her one-bedroom apartment in DC with a prime view of the Jumbotron for Nationals Park. Sister Simone lives in an attractive residential neighborhood in the Southwest Waterfront area of

DC. It is just a 1.6-mile, or about a nine-minute, bike ride to her office on E Street.

I was in the audience when she spoke, to a rousing standing ovation, at the Democratic National Convention in Charlotte, North Carolina, just a couple of months after her appearance on *The Colbert Report*. When DNC organizers first asked her to give a speech, she told them she had three requirements: She wanted to tell the crowd that she was pro-life. She wanted to tell the story of her people, the ones she met on the road. And she wanted to say that everyone was welcome inside her big tent. When they agreed too quickly, Sister Simone thought she probably should have asked for more.

Those in the crowd whispered to one another as she took the podium. Most of the delegates weren't entirely sure who this plain woman approaching the stage, sandwiched on the schedule between the governors of Colorado and Delaware, was. She started by introducing herself: "I'm Sister Simone Campbell, and I'm one of the nuns on the bus. Yes, we have nuns on the bus and a nun at the podium." That broke the ice. Onstage she conveyed a politician's charisma—the Bill Clinton of nuns—coupled with a mother's warmth.

She fairly and pointedly put down Congressman Ryan for exploiting his Catholic faith on the campaign trail. Part of the candidate's stump speech focused on how his Catholicism nurtured his individualistic pull-yourself-up-by-the-bootstraps philosophy. "Paul Ryan says this budget is in keeping with the moral values of our shared faith. I disagree," Sister Simone said, to rousing applause. She touted the truth she had learned along her trip: "Together we understand that an immoral budget that hurts already-struggling families does not reflect our nation's values. We are better than that. I urge you. Join us on the bus." She ended her speech with the crowd already on its feet. "This is what Nuns on the Bus are all about. We care for the Hundred Percent."

Sister Simone later told me that she had been prepared to be ignored up there. "They told me to be ready to just talk over the hum of the arena, but when I got up there, it went silent."

"Holy moly," said the voice in her head when she was onstage. "They're actually listening to me."

Delaware governor Jack Markell came up to her in the green room after her speech.

"I hear you're a tough act to follow," he said.

"No, no, no," Sister Simone responded kindly. "I'm sure you'll do just fine."

Sister Simone carries herself like she is someone you should know, with her shoulders back, chest proud, and a stride of military precision. She shouldn't have been surprised when later that day a group of teenagers stopped her on one of the streets of downtown Charlotte. "You're Sister Simone Campbell!" They jumped up and down with excitement and asked to take a picture. "You're one of the people we wanted to meet at the convention."

NETWORK's Nuns on the Bus began their journey, one that would span nine states and 2,700 miles, stopping in homeless shelters, food pantries, and health-care facilities for the poor, on June 18, 2012.

Their bus driver, Bill, the owner of a silvery mullet and an ever-present Journey T-shirt, had actually spent the previous summer driving the remaining members of that very anthem rock band across the country. I wondered how the gig with the nuns compared with driving around a bus full of aging rock stars.

"A little different," Bill said with a shrug when I asked. "No drugs. And it's quiet. Other than that, no difference. They are some nice ladies."

They kicked off the road trip outside the Fort Des Moines Hotel (where the nuns were offered free rooms) in Des Moines, Iowa. Rekha Basu of the *Des Moines Register* noted that from up the street it looked like a rock band had stopped in town. "Except rock stars wouldn't be up that early," she said. Swarms of people crowded the sidewalks, including reporters bumping up against one another, hoping to get a clear shot of the women as they climbed off the bus.

"Even the moniker had an edgy feel to it—sort of like 'Popes in the piazza,' from the days of Father Guido Sarducci on *Saturday Night Live*," Ms. Basu said. Mature women in the crowd held up large signs written in magic marker: YOU GO GIRLS and ALL FOR NUNS, NUNS FOR ALL.

The tour's first stop was at the Ames office of Rep. Steve King (R-IA), a supporter of Congressman Ryan's budget. The nuns planned to present the congressman's staff with a copy of *The Faithful Budget*, an interfaith, economically sound approach to the country's deficit reduction program drafted by a consortium of Christian, Jewish, and Muslim religious organizations, which called for increased aid to the poor and cuts in military spending.

They had made an appointment at Representative King's, but when they arrived, the congressman's office was shuttered and empty, with a typed note attached to the glass door that read, "Out in the field with constituents. Not available."

Sister Simone slid a copy of the budget underneath his door. It wouldn't be the first time they were snubbed by Republican lawmakers along the way.

The fans wildly outnumbered the enemies, but the nuns did encounter some naysayers on the road. One local abortion foe in Iowa posted an online diatribe against the traveling nuns: "Sorry, Sisters . . . affirming people in their sodomite sin, promoting the slaughter of the innocent preborn, and being in arrogant disobedience to the church (and by extension, to God himself) is scandalous and utterly anti-Catholic."

Coming face-to-face with Rep. Paul Ryan was a priority, and the sisters made their first attempt in Wisconsin at the candidate's hometown office in Janesville. They were greeted by plucky members of his staff who told them that Congressman Ryan was not available. The nuns handed a female staff member a copy of *The Faithful Budget*.

"I had no idea the beauty of this city. I had no idea the size of this city. I am clearly a person from out of town," Sister Simone told the crowd outside of the lawmaker's office as news outlets swarmed her. She charmed them with her easy smile. "We've driven through this fabulous farm country. Farmers know what it is like to be part of a community. You can't do this stuff alone." One supporter there was in awe of the fact that she found herself attending a rally in support of nuns at all. "When I was in Catholic school, nuns were not my heroes and I never thought I would see the day where I forgave them and they were my total heroes," she said. It was a frequent occurrence that members of the crowd would find themselves surprised to be at an event in support of nuns. One of the things that the nuns heard over and over again on the road was, "I'm not religious, but I love your message."

Congressman Ryan was in DC that day and issued a statement defending his budget plan against the Nuns on the Bus: "Economic stagnation, and a growing dependency on government assistance, continues to push this country toward a debt crisis, in which those who get hurt the first and the worst are the poor, the sick and the elderly, the people who need government the most."

Early on, the sisters discovered the importance of centering themselves before beginning each day's journey, in order to keep from getting on one another's nerves.

"We prayed a half hour together every single day before we got going. It was essential," Sister Simone said. "The one day that we missed prayer, we were gnawing on each other in the first hour. Everyone was tense and we weren't connected."

From then on, no matter how late the sisters stayed up at night or how early they had to rise in the morning, often before the sun, they made sure to put in their thirty minutes of group prayer and meditation. "A lot of it was just letting go of control and all the pesky influences the ego brings about," Sister Simone said.

On the road, the nuns continued to spend their time with the poor, the sick, and the elderly—the ones who did indeed need the government the most right at that moment. Unlike Congressman Ryan in his ivory Capitol, the sisters spent their time on the margins of society, just as the Gospel preached. It was about bearing witness. It was about being present in a way that politicians have long stopped being present. "I can't tell you how many people we have cried with," Sister Simone told me. "When I get to be with them, I can tell you that I will never forget them, and in return, they get to know that they aren't alone."

This sense of being with the people who need her help the most is integral to Sister Simone's faith. When I asked her about her connection to God, she hesitated and told me it is hard for her to speak about it in any way that would make sense. She described it as this intuitive and yet odd thing. What she knows is that she feels a deep connection to God when she is in the presence of the people she feels called to serve.

"When we are faithful," she said, "we have to let our hearts be broken by the people around us, and if we let our hearts be broken open, we can feel the deeper call of the Gospel. That's what the bus was about, broken hearts."

Sister Simone collected people's stories on the way, and she can recite them all from memory. The names of the people she met on the road fly off her tongue like individual prayers. Billy, Matt, Mark, Jini . . .

In Milwaukee, Sister Simone met Billy, his wife, and their two boys at the dining room of St. Benedict the Moor Church. Billy's work hours had been slashed in the recession. Being the man of the family, he wanted to step up and take responsibility, but without help from food stamps and the local church, he and his wife had no way to put food on their table. Sister Simone held him in her prayers.

In Toledo they met ten-year-old twins Matt and Mark, who had gotten into trouble at school for fighting. A nun named Sister Virginia and the staff at the Padua Center there, took them into their program when they were suspended to try to figure out what was going on with these little boys who were under so much stress. They wanted to find a solution to the problem before things got even worse. During a home visit, Sister Virginia discovered that these ten-year-olds were trying to care for their bedridden mother with multiple sclerosis and diabetes all on their own. They were her only caregivers. The nuns got the boys' mother medical help and worked to give the twins a sense of stability and childhood. Sister Simone prayed with them.

In Cincinnati, she met Jini Kai, who had arrived straight from her sister Margaret Kistler's memorial service two hours earlier. When Margaret lost her job, she also lost her health insurance. Their father had been diagnosed with colon cancer in his forties; she knew it was likely hereditary but couldn't afford tests and treatment out of pocket. Living without preventative treatment for the disease was the equivalent of a death sentence for Margaret.

"Even as she felt herself growing sicker and sicker," Jini told Sister Simone, referring to Margaret, "she kept her worries to herself. She knew she was in no position to pay for the care she knew she needed.

"When she could no longer walk far enough to answer her front door, a friend scooped her up and they headed for the ER. There her stage-four colon cancer was diagnosed, having already spread to her lungs and liver. It was a diagnosis too late."

Sister Simone listened to Jini's story. She hugged her. She now carries a picture of Margaret tucked away in the Bible she takes with her on the road.

Just a few days into the tour, the bus erupted into cheers and tears of joy as the nuns were gathered around the bus's television and learned that the Affordable Care Act was upheld by the Supreme Court.

"My immediate reaction was elation mixed with relief and a sense that riding beside me were the hundreds of people I had met during our bus journey—people who, like me, would be directly impacted by this historic decision," Sister Simone told me.

Sister Simone has always been political.

In the second grade, when a proposition threatened funding for Catholic schools in her Southern California hometown, she organized her fellow neighborhood children to demonstrate. Her father, an aeronautical engineer for the Douglas Aircraft Company with a fondness for gadgetry, bought one of the first televisions in the neighborhood, which allowed Simone and her sister to watch political conventions and the rise of Dr. Martin Luther King in the living room of their ranch-style house.

"Dr. King was our hero. We just couldn't understand why kids would have to have guards to go to school," she told me. "That made civil rights feel real to me."

Like many Catholic kids in the 1950s and '60s, Simone dreamed of being a missionary, traveling to exotic lands and serving the poor.

"In my more noble thoughts, I imagined I would be a doctor. I liked the idea of caring for people," she told me with a laugh. "I don't think I thought it through very well, though." She felt changed after she made her First Communion in second grade. It was a feeling of freedom that never really left her.

Becoming a nun was simply the sensible solution for Simone, and she describes her journey to the sisterhood as organic rather than dramatic. It was while organizing a sit-in at the Board of Education at Immaculate Heart College in Los Angeles that she decided it would be her calling.

"Faith was about justice for me. I was thinking that I do this kind of work because of my faith, but no one ever talked about that. I grew up in California, for heaven's sake. Nobody ever talked about faith there. I wanted my life to be about both, justice and faith. From then on, I couldn't imagine being anything but a Sister of Social Service," she said. The Sisters of Social Service are one of the most progressive communities of vowed women out there. They are a cadre of badass women, starting with their founder, Sister Margaret Slachta, who would later go on to become the first female parliamentarian in Hungary at the turn of the twentieth century. The first three Social Service sisters in America lived a bohemian life in a small house on West Second Street in Bunker Hill in Los Angeles. They eschewed the traditional long black veils and convent living well before the changes of Vatican II, in favor of simple gray dresses and living among the poor. Like Sister Simone, they were seen daily on the streets visiting families and finding food and clothing for the very poor. Well known among the order is the story of Sister Sára Salkaházi, who ran a safe house for Jews during World War II. On December 27, 1944, members of the pro-Nazi Arrow Cross movement arrested Sister Sára and the Jewish women sheltered there, whom she refused to abandon. She was taken to the banks of the Danube, where the group of them were all stripped and shot.

After finishing her bachelor's degree, Sister Simone began her first year of work as a social worker on the glittery streets of Beverly Hills, working with drug-addicted teenagers and domestic workers. She received her JD at the University of California at Davis before founding and serving as the lead attorney for the Community Law Center in Oakland, California, which charged on a sliding scale based on a client's income. Afterward, she served as general director of the Sisters of Social Service and then as executive director of JERICHO, a California advocacy and education organization that served those living at the economic margins.

In 2004, right in the middle of George W. Bush's presidency, she accepted a position as executive director of NETWORK, the Catholic social justice lobbying group in

Washington, DC. She tried for four years to get a meeting with that president's White House Office of Faith-Based and Community Initiatives, but without any success. Founded on December 17, 1971, NETWORK was the brainchild of forty-seven Catholic sisters across the country who came together to lobby for federal policies and legislation promoting economic justice. In April 1972, they opened a two-person office that became the epicenter for Washington-area Catholic peace and justice activism. Their justice agenda ranged from global hunger to nuclear weapons and women's rights, and their legislative seminars drew activists and politicians from around the globe, including such prominent members of Congress as Ted Kennedy, Adlai Stevenson, Walter Mondale, and Joe Biden.

In the spring of 2012, the organization had just celebrated its fortieth anniversary. That is when, as Sister Simone described it, the Holy Spirit began to make some mischief with them. Four days later they were named in an official Vatican document as a "suspect organization" that was a bad influence on American nuns.

"We're only a nine-person staff and we made the Vatican nervous. *Holy moly!*" she said with a laugh when we talked about it later that year. The Holy See's hand slap was due to Sister Simone's and NETWORK's support of President Barack Obama's health care legislation. The Catholic sisters had split from the thinking of the American Catholic bishops who opposed the Affordable Care Act on the grounds that it would allow federal funding for abortions. The nuns believed a different analysis that said the bill would *not* provide federal funding for abortions.

The nuns refused to let this difference of opinion jettison a plan that could have such a huge impact on the poor. They knew President Obama's health-care overhaul would provide coverage to hundreds of thousands of Americans who'd previously been unable to afford it. Sister Simone wrote the famous "nuns' letter," signed by leaders of Catholic Sisters who supported the Affordable Care Act.

We have witnessed firsthand the impact of our national health care crisis, particularly its impact on women, children and people who are poor. We see the toll on families who have delayed seeking care due to a lack of health insurance coverage or lack of funds with which to pay high deductibles and co-pays. We have counseled and prayed with men, women and children who have been denied health care coverage by insurance companies. We have witnessed early and avoidable deaths because of delayed medical treatment. . . . While it is an imperfect measure, it is a crucial next step in realizing health care for all. It will invest in preventative care. It will bar insurers from denying coverage based on pre-existing conditions. It will make crucial investments in community health centers that largely serve poor women and children. And despite false claims to the contrary, the Senate bill will not provide taxpayer funding for elective abortions. It will *uphold longstanding conscience protections and it will make historic new investments—$250 million—in support of pregnant women. This is the REAL pro-life stance and we as Catholics are all for it.*

"The girls played the boys, and for once the girls won, and the boys were pissed," Sister Simone told me, clapping her hands together with great joy in her voice. "It's all politics."

The Vatican's censure made her even feistier. Unfortunately, the sisters didn't have enough cash on hand to make a big, expensive splash.

When Sister Simone has a problem to solve, she takes to prayer. She prays and meditates for an hour each morning, facilitated by an egg timer and a prayer cushion. When she is home, she gets to do it in a designated corner of her apartment. On the wall above the little nook are things that make her happy, mostly gifts: an eye of God from the Dominican sisters in Iraq, a photograph of her fellow sisters, and an icon of Saint Peter, her patron saint. She prayed that spring with all of NETWORK and gathered a group of big thinkers in Washington to a summit where they discussed how they could get their name out there within the constraints of their limited budget.

"It's a sign of the Holy Spirit that no one remembers who said it first, especially in a city where everyone loves to claim credit, but someone said 'road trip,' and by the end of the meeting it was clear that we would go on the road in a wrapped bus. I had no idea what a wrapped bus was, but I knew it would lift up our mission of two years pushing against the Paul Ryan budget," Sister Simone said. A map of the places they would visit had already formed in her mind.

I joined the nun bus in June, in the town adjacent to the one I grew up in, five minutes from my Catholic high school, Villa Joseph Marie. It was roomier than I expected and had wireless Internet, a flat-screen television, three bunks on each side, and comfortable seats. But it was still a bus—no more than 100 square feet of space for up to twelve people at a time.

A digital thermometer at the suburban shopping center in Newtown, Pennsylvania, hit 103 degrees on a Friday afternoon as the nuns' sky-blue vehicle pulled into the parking lot. The word NUNS was writ large in red, immediately informing the casual passerby that this was holier than your average bus. Sweat pooled on the upper lips and brows of the nearly one hundred supporters gathered on the black asphalt. When the nuns emerged, they were cool as cucumbers. The bus had excellent air conditioning.

They *were* cool, generally, the group of Catholic sisters that Sister Simone had assembled.

There was Mary Ellen Lacy, a Daughter of Charity who previously provided legal services to residents along the Gulf Coast after Hurricane Katrina and the BP oil spill. She now works as an immigration attorney, but at various points in her life she has been a lobbyist and a nurse.

Diane Donaghue was a spry eighty-one-year-old. When I asked her if she thought she would still be making bus trips at age eighty-two, she didn't hesitate. "Why wouldn't I?" she said, like it was an incredibly silly question to even ask.

The reporter in Iowa was right about the way the crowd in that parking lot went wild. There was a kind of rock-star quality to it all, one that appealed to middle-aged women in Dockers and sensible shoes.

The Nuns on the Bus, they feed the poor, feed the poor, feed the poor; the Nuns on the Bus, they feed the poor through the United States. The group sang along to a bastardized version of "The Wheels on the Bus," adding two extra syllables to "through" so that it sounded like "thooo-ooo-roo."

The Nuns on the Bus say reject Ryan's budget, reject Ryan's budget, reject Ryan's budget; the Nuns on the Bus say reject Ryan's budget through the United States.

The Nuns on the Bus say we are mad, we are mad, we are mad; the Nuns on the Bus say we are mad . . .

It went on.

Days later, in Virginia, Sister Simone and her fellow nuns attempted to get up close and personal with House Majority Leader Eric Cantor at his local headquarters in an office park in a suburb of Richmond.

Just reaching Cantor's office was a struggle for the bus. Destructive weather, including tornadoes, wreaked havoc on the Virginia countryside that weekend. Roads were flooded and trees were ripped from the ground by their roots. I considered bailing on the trip.

"Be careful," Sister Simone e-mailed me. "But I hope we get to see you."

She and the sisters were beyond determined to reach just the parking lot of the congressman's office, never mind getting inside.

"We said this was a stop we had to make because of how important Mr. Cantor is right now and how he is missing so much of the story that is happening in America," Sister Simone told me. Her fellow nuns, whom she referred to without irony as her "peeps" and members of her "posse," nodded aggressively in agreement. "We want to tell these stories on Capitol Hill. So often these folks on Capitol Hill are disconnected, and they want us to believe people are lazy and dependent. They are not lazy and they are not dependent."

As with the entire trip, that meeting was mostly about being as present as possible.

"I didn't expect him to come, but we needed to come. We needed to be here to say I had seen his office and I've seen his people," Sister Simone told me outside. "We had to come to Cantor's office because Cantor is a key player, second in command in the House, and he has scuttled a couple of key steps forward for our nation that Speaker Boehner thought were a good idea that then got scuttled for other political reasons. We've got to wake him up. This is not a game."

Later that afternoon we visited the Shalom Farm, a cooperative community that grows food to feed the needy. Sister Richelle Friedman, who had grown up on a farm in Iowa, took a turn driving the tractor.

The final stop on the tour was Washington, DC, at a stage erected in front of the graceful United Methodist Building, catty-corner to the US Capitol. As the nuns arrived, they ran— to the theme from *Rocky*, no less—through a scrum of fans, shaking hands and giving hugs. Security guards in dark black sunglasses looked important as they kept the crowd at bay.

"The Nuns on the Bus tour comes to a close today, but by no means are we finished standing up to the misguided politicians who will harm people on the margins of society," Sister Simone said to deafening applause in front of a large American flag. "We will not be silent."

"Get your T-shirts, Nuns on the Bus T-shirts here," yelled a pimply-faced kid barely into his twenties, a devotee of Nuns on the Bus and a true capitalist who printed his own I'M WITH THE NUNS T-shirts and sold them for $15 apiece. The shirts, like concert tees, had a list of the cities the nuns visited: Des Moines, Janesville, Milwaukee, Toledo, and Cincinnati. They sold out in an hour.

Sister Simone was energized onstage, pumping her fist in the air.

She was exhausted by the time she left it.

"What next?" I asked.

"I want to do my laundry and take a shower," she said with a smile.

After all that, Paul Ryan finally agreed to a meeting. He asked that no media be informed or allowed to attend the one-on-one engagement at his Capitol Hill office.

"He spent most of his time trying to impress me," Sister Simone said when we discussed it later. During their brief time together, he boasted to the nun, trying to wow her with his asceticism, saying he often slept overnight on a cot in his office.

"Is that good for you, or for your family?" Sister Simone responded. It's just not possible to out-Catholic a nun. He quickly changed the subject.

"I was looking to build a connection, so I proposed that we both say we care passionately about the future of our nation, and he just said, 'Yeah,'" she told me. "He just really lives inside his own head. It is so sad." She joined the congressman on a walk across the Capitol's grassy lawn to his next meeting. Their good-bye was stilted and cordial.

When she got back to her simple brick office on E Street, she penned Ryan a note saying that she hoped after the election the two of them could sit down and try to find some common ground. She waited for a response.

From there, the Nuns on the Bus movement took on a life of its own. In September, more than two hundred nuns gathered at the Whitehall Ferry Terminal in Lower Manhattan for a protest called "Nuns on the Ferry."

"We were told that a bus is no big deal in New York," said Sister Mary Ellen. "So somebody said, 'Could they get on a ferry?'" They certainly could.

"The idea for the ferry was that the Paul Ryan budget was in Never Never Land, so we should ride a *ferry*," Sister Simone said, underscoring how "ferry" sounds like "fairy." "It makes sense."

To get to the ferry terminal, Sister Simone had taken the A train into Manhattan from the Daughters of Charity House in the Bedford-Stuyvesant neighborhood of Brooklyn. "It was Nuns on the Subway," she cracked when I met up with her at the terminal.

"We need to do Nuns on the Train," Sister Mary Ellen interjected.

"We should go interfaith," Sister Simone countered. "Rabbis on Roller Skates." They both buckled into laughter. Nun jokes.

In October, Sister Simone saw off another group of nuns who opted to tour more than 1,000 miles in Ohio in time for the presidential debate between Paul Ryan and the sitting vice president, Joe Biden. There in the Buckeye State they received some of the most vitriolic protests of the trip. An angry local Tea Party affiliate prayed the Rosary and shook their fists, calling out the women as "fake nuns." They wielded signs labeling the tour THE HIGHWAY TO HELL and BUMS ON THE BUS.

Sister Simone thought that was it, the end of the road, as they say. But in 2013, the Holy Spirit continued to make mischief with the nuns and they set out on their grandest trip yet, returning to the Hudson River Basin to kick off a Nuns on the Bus reboot near Ellis Island, this time focusing on immigration reform and traveling more than 6,800 miles through fifteen states in three weeks. They would travel down the East Coast, across the South, and then up through California, ending at Marina Park in San Francisco, overlooking Angel Island and Alcatraz. The journey was more difficult this time for many reasons, the least of which was the length of the trip. If the first Nuns on the Bus trip broke Sister Simone's heart, this one cracked it wide open and made it bleed.

"I wasn't prepared for how painful it was going to be," she said, her voice breaking. "The last time, we went out to prevent bad things from happening. With this trip, we had to lift up the stories of horrible things that had already happened. There was a whole different level of anguish to it."

There were more stories, more names, more broken hearts.

It was also the first trip that brought the nuns to the southern part of the United States, an area that Sister Simone, a woman who had traveled around the world, including to war zones in Lebanon, Syria, and Iraq, had never spent much time in and a place where she was challenged to face her own prejudices.

"The South makes me nervous. I grew up with it being

so racist and segregated. When I first moved to DC, I realized that I had a prejudice against white men speaking with Southern accents. It was something I had to confront on the trip."

Writing for *Politico* at the end of 2013, Nancy Pelosi, the minority leader for the House of Representatives, called Sister Simone a "champion for the cause of peace and justice." She continued: "There are qualities that define Sister Simone—and that make her an inspiration to millions of Americans, Catholic and non-Catholic alike. These are the characteristics that remind each of us of our own responsibilities to speak up, to judge others fairly, to defend the rights of the poor and needy. These are the values that Sister Simone drives home, on a bus and in our communities— and that we should each strive to live by each day, in Congress and in our country."

Every day, Sister Simone prays to be enough for the people who depend on her. During her time on the bus, she wrote a poem based on the story of the loaves and fishes recounted in all four Gospels. In that ancient story, which is the only miracle besides the resurrection that is featured in all of the Gospels, Jesus feeds a multitude of the poor— 5,000 people—by blessing five barley loaves and two small fish. The crowd eats from the broken pieces, and the hungry soon find themselves full. The moral of the story in its simplest version is that you can do an awful lot with just a little.

Sister Simone's poem begins like this: "I always joked

that the miracle of the loaves and fish was sharing. The women always know this."

At the end of the verse is her favorite line: "Blessed and broken, you are enough. I savor the blessed, cower at the broken and pray to be enough."

"It tells the story of how we are all in such lonely places and how we all need to be fed," Sister Simone said, mentioning again her need to be present with the people. "We need to feed each other, and you can't do that feeding on e-mail. You can do some of it, but it is not enough nourishment."

The Nuns on the Bus covered more than 10,000 miles of the US in two years. I asked Sister Simone if they would just keep going, if there would always be new battles for the nun bus to fight.

At first she joked. "We created some car magnets, so you can have nuns on the bus too. There are guidelines on our website. The rule is you have to have at least one nun."

But then she grew serious.

"I don't understand it myself," she told me. "But there continues to be this hunger for whatever the bus is. I never thought there would be a second one, but the country needed it. I like to say that the bus is like Robin Hood; it will show up whenever you need it. People are hungry for it. Everyone wants to know that they are not in this alone."

Being in her presence is invigorating. She has an irresistible confidence that makes you want to be an active participant in whatever call to action she is advocating at that moment. She is also thoughtful and kind, even over the phone. As we finished up a phone interview one afternoon, I developed a terrible cough. Sister Simone was frustrated.

"I wish I was there with you to give you a lozenge right now," she said with genuine concern. Given her ability to accomplish seemingly impossible tasks, I thought she would somehow actually reach through the line to hand me a Halls.

During our many conversations, Sister Simone shrugged off suggestions that she should run for political office with a roll of her eyes, and yet I could tell that she didn't discount these suggestions entirely. Her supporters beg her to do it, even though she often refers to the inside of government as a "sausage-making pressure cooker." They have minted bumper stickers that read RUN SISTER RUN: SISTER SIMONE FOR OFFICE.

"Apparently people don't care which office I run for, as long as I run," she told me. She smiled then and glanced away, thinking for a moment. "I think I may be a better nudge on government from the outside, but you never know."

One day between Christmas and New Year's Eve in 2013, she asked me, "You know what I would really like to do?" She had a new haircut since we last talked. It was about four inches longer, in a chic bob that swept along the curve of her chin. One of the makeup artists at MSNBC told her that the audience often found women with longer hair more believable. As a lawyer, Sister Simone is always skeptical of statements like that, but she grew her hair out anyhow. She blushed when I told her how pretty it made her look.

"I can't even imagine what you are going to say," I replied with a grin.

"I have heard a rumor that Frank will be visiting Philadelphia in 2015," she said. I already knew that she referred to the new Pope Francis colloquially as Frank, as if they had graduated from a first-name relationship to the kind of friendship that warrants nicknames. She never said it in a disrespectful way. I think that she did it as a way of making him seem more human, more like one of her peeps. "I would love to get him on the bus. Do you think we could do it?"

I thought about it for a minute. If anyone could get Pope Frank on a bus with a group of women, it would probably be Sister Simone.

3.

It Isn't About Being Gay; It's About Being in Love

Lesbian and gay people have been marginalized because of their orientation. They are denied basic human dignity. It is a clear affront to the social justice teachings of the Church.

—Sister Jeannine Gramick

How could Sister Jeannine Gramick have known that meeting a handsome gay stranger named Dominic at a house party on Spruce Street in West Philadelphia would completely change the course of her life?

It was 1969, and Jeannine was a doctoral candidate in mathematics at the University of Pennsylvania. She was only a few years into her tenure as a Catholic nun, living at the convent of Sisters of the Holy Child Jesus at Thirty-Eighth and Chestnut Streets, on the night she encountered the attractive young man at a joint liturgy shared by a Catholic priest and an Episcopal priest at a home near the school. Interfaith ceremonies back then were organized religion's way of loosening up, trying to get in line with the rest of the long-haired, bell-bottomed decade, and Sister Jeannine was intrigued by the diverse crowds that assembled and the exciting ideas that bubbled up in a melting pot of Christian faiths. At a small reception afterward, guests were encouraged to mingle and chat over passed cheeses and meats. That's where Dominic strode up to her. He was a baptized gay man who had left the Catholic Church because a priest told him that he was going to hell. He wasn't alone. Most of his circle of gay friends hadn't set foot in a church for years for the same reason.

Dominic's story made the young nun squirm. She knew there was a profound stigma against homosexuality, especially in conservative Philadelphia, but she despised the idea that the Church would exclude anyone for something so inconsequential. Dominic asked Sister Jeannine if she would be willing to host a home liturgy for him and his buddies, telling her he missed his faith and the Church. Anxious to help, to do something to heal his wounds, she agreed.

"I got a priest friend of mine to come to Dominic's apartment and we had about a dozen men there. Many of them hadn't been to church in years. They were so stunned that there would be a sister and a priest there who would welcome them. They were so shy at first," Sister Jeannine remembered. "There was this feeling of great exhilaration, great joy. We made them feel very loved. We made them feel like they weren't flawed." They continued the practice once a week . . . mostly at Dominic's house and sometimes at other people's houses. It became known as the home liturgy group for the gay community.

Sister Jeannine didn't start out so open-minded. Following the Catholic mindset at the time, she thought gay people had something wrong with them, that they were sick. She struggled against her own prejudices and apprehensions to keep the events going. "I didn't know what to expect. I thought I had never met any gay people before in my life and I was just a little nervous," she recalled. "But after I got to know them, I didn't think these people were sick at all."

What struck Sister Jeannine the most was their gratitude for her service. "They just had this sense of amazement that there would be church people interested in them."

She repeated to them over and over, "This is your church too." After a while they started to believe her.

The events were such a success that Dominic and his friends wanted more, and he kept nudging her to do something bigger.

"What is the Catholic Church doing for my gay brothers and sisters?" he would demand after their meetings.

"Nothing," she admitted guiltily.

In the early 1970s, gay rights were still a marginal civil rights issue. The Stonewall riots, the demonstrations in New York's Greenwich Village, only just happened in 1969. In 1971, Colorado and Oregon repealed sodomy laws. Idaho had repealed its sodomy law but reinstated it because it couldn't take the backlash from Mormons and Catholics. The American Psychiatric Association didn't remove homosexuality from its list of psychiatric disorders until 1973. As for the Catholic Church, its stance on gays was hard and fast. The official Vatican position was the same then as it is today in 2014: being gay is morally neutral; flawed, but morally neutral. The belief was that in the best of possible scenarios, God wouldn't have created homosexuals at all. However, God *did* make homosexuals, and His creation shouldn't be censured. Any type of homosexual activity, however, is viewed as a sin. That's the reason Dominic and his friends were thrown out of confessional booths when they revealed the things they had done in the privacy of their bedrooms. The story of gay rights in the Catholic Church represents a kind of xenophobia at the core of the institution, a fear and castigation of the unknown.

Sister Jeannine did her research, hungrily reading anything she could get her hands on that touched on the intersection of homosexuality and Catholicism. One of the theories she dove into came from the moral theologian Fr. Charles Curran, a Roman Catholic priest with two doctorates in theology from Rome. In the early '70s Curran contended that homosexual acts, in the context of a committed relationship, may not be the ideal, but they were both good and healthy for homosexual individuals.

There are sections of scripture that Sister Jeannine still looks to today that illustrate God's inclusiveness. She points to Saint Paul's letter to the Galatians, 3:28.

"There is neither Jew nor Greek, there is neither slave nor free man, there is neither male nor female; for you are all one in Christ Jesus. And if you belong to Christ, then you are Abraham's descendants, heirs according to promise."

"He didn't say gay or straight in there, but that is the implication," Sister Jeannine said. "These things shouldn't divide us. God doesn't see the world through a lens of gender, sexuality, or ethnicity. To me that is a wonderful bit of the scripture."

She cites the story of David and his friendship with Jonathan, the two rivals for the throne of Israel who forged a deep friendship and loving bond:

Now it came about when he had finished speaking to Saul, that the soul of Jonathan was knit to the soul of David, and Jonathan loved him as himself. Saul took him that day and did not let him return to his father's house. Then

Jonathan made a covenant with David because he loved him as himself. Jonathan stripped himself of the robe that was on him and gave it to David, with his armor, including his sword and his bow and his belt. So David went out wherever Saul sent him, and prospered; and Saul set him over the men of war.

Sister Jeannine doesn't come right out and say that the relationship between David and Jonathan was necessarily a physical or sexual one, "But it was certainly a same-sex love," Sister Jeannine told me. "It is about people of the same gender loving each other. It is good to point to these scriptures because people always emphasize sex, sex, sex. And it isn't about sex. It is about love. It is who you fall in love with that makes you lesbian and gay. Love is the important thing here, not sex."

As her home liturgies became more popular, Dominic arranged for Sister Jeannine to give an interview to the *Philadelphia Bulletin*. He just cold-called the editor of the paper and said, "I have an interview lined up for you." What good newspaperman could resist a story about a good-looking young-local-girl-turned-nun hanging around with a bunch of gay guys? As a journalist, that is the kind of cold call I have always loved.

Next to a portrait of the charmingly posed nun, beautiful in her sleeveless white blouse, a simple black skirt, and a movie star's smile, was the headline: "A Nun in Any

Clothes Is Still a Nun." My favorite paragraph from the four-hundred-word piece is the lede: "She plays guitar. She's also pretty, and is 29 years old today. She believes people should do their own thing. She does. And she thinks everyone should be tolerant of human difference."

Sister Jeannine told the reporter, "I'm interested in anyone, but my most recent apostolate is meeting and working with gay people. . . . At first it was just a matter of being friendly, like I am to anyone, but now I guess my goal is to try to make people feel less uptight like they do when they hear the word homosexual. It's very unchristian." She is flip and cool in all of her answers. The reporter asks her about her liberal attitude toward wearing the nun's habit. She replies. "I wear clothes appropriate to the occasion. If I'm going to the beach, I wear a bathing suit. If I'm going on a picnic, I'm apt to wear a short 'scooter' skirt."

Sister Jeannine was on pins and needles when the article first came out. "I expected a negative reaction," she said to me after she had pulled the clipping out of her archives. But she was pleasantly surprised. "I received a couple dozen letters, two-thirds of them from Catholics who supported what I was doing."

Sister Jeannine would continue her home ministry for the remainder of the year before leaving Philadelphia for Baltimore in 1972 to teach math at Notre Dame of Maryland.

Dominic would go on to make a name for himself at the

forefront of Philadelphia's gay activist community while running a successful salon called the Abbey in South Philly. The name reflected how deeply connected Sister Jeannine helped him feel to his Catholic faith. On the day he went to get his license to cut hair in the state of Pennsylvania, she was his hair model. He loved making people look fabulous, himself included, particularly as his platinum-blond drag persona, Madominic, who was partial to sequined leotards and lavender feather boas. When Sister Jeannine left Philly, Dominic extended their ministry to AIDS patients, visiting them as a spiritual guide several times a week. He served communion during his visits, counseled the patients, and helped them organize funeral services. Dominic succumbed to the disease himself on January 24, 1993.

Word traveled fast among the religious communities back then—not as fast as on Twitter and Facebook today, but swiftly all the same—and just about every nun on the Eastern seaboard knew what Sister Jeannine was up to with her gay ministry. Her community of Sisters of Notre Dame was impressed with it and assigned her to work full-time in gay and lesbian ministry in Maryland, an incredibly liberal decision for the School Sisters of Notre Dame to make, one completely without precedent and filled with risk for the entire community. "When we first began, my role was tenuous," Sister Jeannine told me. "There was skepticism in the Catholic community. No one in the Catholic community had been assigned to gay ministry before. It wasn't even a thing. People were anxious about any sexual issues, much less homosexual ones. Those superiors were women of vision. They stood by me."

Sister Jeannine could grapple all day long with conservative Catholics over homophobia and heterosexism. But that wasn't the story she wanted to tell. Her fight was about exclusion. It was about civil rights. She knew that she needed to flip the script and pivot from a focus on sexual ethics to a narrative about social justice.

"Lesbian and gay people have been marginalized because of their orientation. They are denied basic human dignity," Sister Jeannine told me with an angry tinge to her voice. "It is a clear affront to the social justice teachings of the Church."

She added with a chuckle, "If we were going to fire every person whose life is not in line with the sexual ethics of the Church, we wouldn't have many people in the Catholic institution."

While the Church at large maintained an anti-homosexual stance, splinter groups throughout the institution were starting to consider "the gay issue." Sister Jeannine was not venturing into this territory alone. In 1976, Bishop Francis J. Mugavero of Brooklyn wrote one of the first Roman Catholic statements to contain a compassionate and encouraging message to gay and lesbian people. Entitled "Sexuality: God's Gift," it offered that gay and lesbian people deserved to be treated equally in society generally and in the Christian community. Mugavero, tall, bald, and staunchly liberal, spoke directly to the homosexual community in his letter: "We pledge our willingness . . . to try to find new ways to communicate the truth of Christ because we believe it will make you free."

That passage, and that phrase "new ways," caught Sister Jeannine's attention. There had to be a new way, she thought. Soon there would be. One of the letters Sister Jeannine received after that newspaper article ran in the *Bulletin* came from a local Philadelphia priest, Fr. Bob Nugent.

Father Bob said in his letter, "If there is anything I can do to help, just let me know." Sister Jeannine wrote back: "We need priests to preside at the Eucharist." So he joined her in her home ministries. Father Bob would later call this their Adam and Eve story, because Sister Jeannine was the one who gave him the apple. He thought it was a humorous way to say "The nun made me do it!"

By 1976, Father Bob had left Philadelphia for Washington, DC, where he was working at the Quixote Center, a Maryland-based Catholic social justice group. He called Sister Jeannine about an opening on the staff, saying the center wanted to start a program on justice for lesbian and gay Catholics. She joined, but after a year she and Father Bob realized there was enough work for an entire justice organization solely devoted to gay and lesbian issues and the practicality of living as a gay Catholic. And so in 1977, borrowing the phrase from Mugavero's letter, they started New Ways Ministry and devoted themselves to making life easier for Catholic gays and lesbians.

Up until the day she met Dominic, Sister Jeannine had thought she would spend her life as a math teacher. She loved teaching math, loved the order and the elegance of proofs and equations.

"I still miss teaching math," she said, "but many people could teach math, and at that time there was no religious person working on behalf of lesbian and gay Catholics. That was God's call for me. It was what I needed to do."

She recounted a story from that time about an older nun who had no idea what it meant to be homosexual or what "New Ways" was all about. The elderly sister was in the dark about what Sister Jeannine even did with "those people," and why they needed their own special ministry in the first place.

Sister Jeannine patiently explained the basics of homosexuality. The older nun just shook her head.

"I understand now," the older sister replied slowly. "But I think I like the 'Old Ways' better." Sister Jeannine at least had to give her credit for asking.

That was the institutional stance in a nutshell.

Like its name and its co-founders, the vision and philosophy of New Ways was solidly Catholic. Sister Jeannine and Father Bob's work was based firmly in the positive messages of justice, acceptance, dialogue, and reconciliation. Sister Jeannine wanted no less than equality for gays and lesbians in the Church and in the world. Her mission was to educate Catholics that their gay and lesbian brothers and sisters were just like them.

The New Ways mission was all about education. They spent a significant share of their time and resources providing workshops for Church personnel across the country. Entitled "Building Bridges: Gay and Lesbian Christians and the Church," these programs offered positive information on Church pronouncements, scripture interpretation, lesbian/gay spirituality, and pastoral outreach. Gays, lesbians, and their family members and pastoral ministers attended. The structure of the workshops allowed for storytelling and dialogue so that the walls of ignorance and fear could be broken down.

During one of her earliest retreats, Sister Jeannine ran into a close friend of hers from grade school and high school whom she hadn't seen for a decade. The two of them used to dance like crazy with all the boys on the dance floor, but during their walks home, her old friend always told her that she felt like she related to all men like they were her brother. She never understood what that meant until she went off to medical school and fell in love with a woman.

"So I was wrong," Sister Jeannine told me. "I did know gay people when I was growing up. I just didn't know it."

That was the crux of it for her: Show people that there is

nothing different or strange about gay people. Show them that they are their friends and their neighbors. She believed that if New Ways could just break it down for people that this was an issue of exclusion, she would be able to win supporters to her side.

New Ways programs expanded nationwide. They created a retreat program for parents of lesbian and gay children, pilgrimages around the world for lesbian and gay families, and even the Lesbian Sisters Project, a support system for nuns in various stages of coming out to their communities and to their families.

It was a scrappy start. At first they worked out of Father Bob's small apartment, and once that grew too claustrophobic they spilled over into Sister Jeannine's apartment, which wasn't much bigger. In 1980, Sister Jeannine's parents lent them the money to buy a house in Mt. Rainier, Maryland, right on Eastern Avenue, the dividing line between Maryland and Washington, DC. The white stucco three-story with baby-blue trim let them finally give desks to all their interns and grow the organization. They set on publishing book after book: *Homosexuality and the Catholic Church*, *The Vatican and Homosexuality*, *Homosexuality and the Magisterium*—all with the intention of convincing Catholics that gay people belonged to the Church just as much as everyone else. Today Sister Jeannine lives in the attic of that house with her cat, Kitty—a shy, lovable kitten of a cat that weighs in at just seven pounds.

I first visited the New Ways Ministry house a few days after Christmas. Most of the suburban streets were in a state of half-decoration, deflated lawn ornaments littering yards and strings of lights hanging halfheartedly from windows. Sister Jeannine and I made plans for the evening and she e-mailed me to invite me to stay over. "An early dinner sounds fine and then you can have a 'sleep-over' at the nuns' house," she wrote. Just a day before my visit, she got word that Father Bob's health had taken a turn for the worse, and she was rushing to be by the bedside of the priest, who had since relocated to Milwaukee, that night. Still, she carved out a few hours to spend with me, picking me up at the train station in her old black Nissan with the bumper sticker declaring to the state of Maryland: CIVIL MARRIAGE IS A CIVIL RIGHT.

Once we arrived at the New Ways headquarters, Sister Jeannine fussed over me, serving palm-sized scones with butter and Smucker's strawberry jam. An ancient teakettle whistled as she puttered around the warm kitchen, deciding that tea would be easier to serve. Over her fluffy white curls, smoke stains marked the white clapboard cabinet door as proof that this was a kitchen that had been much used and much loved. Sister Jeannine is slight and almost elfin in a blue cardigan two sizes too big with a playful reindeer pattern; roomy black pants; and Teva sandals, the kind you wear white-water rafting, with thick black socks. Kitty spied on me skeptically from the doorway. A much chubbier cat marched brazenly up to me to say hello by shoving his head into my calf.

"That one isn't mine," Sister Jeannine said with a shake of her head as the cat gazed up at her. "He is a neighborhood cat who just comes in here looking for food. We can't get rid of him, and don't want to. We just love him too."

The interloper padded behind us as Sister Jeannine walked me through the old house's foyer, where the history of the organization plays out in photographs lining the walls to create a makeshift New Ways Hall of Fame. One photo showed a pretty woman in her thirties in a simple dress and a shaggy bob haircut, sitting in front of a *Thorn Birds*–handsome priest. "That's Bob and I," she said, beaming at the black-and-white photograph. There were group snapshots of New Ways pilgrims, with Sister Jeannine front and center, holding up a rainbow flag in front of St. Peter's in Rome, the pyramids in Egypt, the Dome of the Rock in Jerusalem, and the Alhambra in Spain. There was the slightly yellowing ad they placed in the *Denver Post* newspaper in 1993 during Pope John Paul II's visit to Colorado, asking for respect for lesbian and gay persons. There was a letter from Sen. Ted Kennedy thanking Father Bob and Sister Jeannine for providing him a copy of their position paper on human dignity and gay rights. "New Ways ministry should be commended for providing creative leadership in this area," the senator from Massachusetts wrote. "I look forward to working with you on these serious and complex issues in the future." In the living room, hanging over comfortable old furniture, was a picture of Sister Jeannine's parents, a pair none too happy to see their only daughter run off to join the convent.

As an only child growing up on Scattergood Street in Northeast Philadelphia, Jeannine first heard God's call to become a nun when she was only seven years old and attending Catholic grade school at St. John Cantius. She was a popular child, well-liked by her peers, but instead of using that popularity for dastardly things as young girls sometimes do, Jeannine imagined she could use other people's affection for her to bring them closer to God.

"I felt that if I identified with a vocation that was God-connected and I was liked by people, then somehow I would be drawing people to God. I hoped that I would be a conduit for God's love. That's what I was thinking about when I was seven." She laughed. One of the things that sets her apart, even among other nuns, is how completely present she is with you at any given moment. She is completely attentive in a way that shows in her eyes and how she touches you when she talks. I had seen it before in celebrities, namely Tom Cruise, who takes the time to make direct eye contact and touch every reporter on the arm as he walks along a red carpet at a movie premiere. It may be one of the reasons the other kids liked Jeannine so much. It is one of the reasons I liked her so much as we sat in her kitchen that cold winter morning. She continued: "I told my mother I was going to be a sister, and she said, 'All Catholic little girls say they want to be sisters when they grow up. You'll grow out of it.'"

The word "devout" lacks a certain seriousness and ferocity in Sister Jeannine's view, so she hates using it. But everyone else described her as a devout child, both serious and ferocious about her faith.

"I went to Mass every day. I said my morning and my night prayers. I was very much in love with God," she said. "In those days, if you really loved God and you were a female, then you became a nun."

She was a hometown girl, a real Philly girl, who only left the city a handful of times on school field trips. St. Hubert's Diocesan High School graduated more than 700 kids the year that she graduated and had 65 nuns on the faculty, all from different orders. Each year Jeannine would become enamored with a different sister and decide that without a doubt she wanted to be in their order. Freshman year, she loved her Latin teacher, so she wanted to be a Mercy nun like her. Sophomore year, she was partial to her religion teacher, a Sister of St. Joseph. Finally, in her junior year, she met a School Sister of Notre Dame—her history teacher and moderator of the debate club. That was the order that stuck.

In that day, girls entered the convent straight out of high school.

"It was time for my serious life's work to begin. I entered

religious life right after high school and I have never, ever regretted it. It is where I should be and where I am meant to be. I have been very happy," she told me. Her mother wasn't so happy. She cried the day Jeannine entered the convent, lamenting that she would never get to be a grandmother.

Sitting at her kitchen table, I asked Sister Jeannine if she ever regretted not having a husband or kids. She didn't flinch.

"Not at all! That wasn't my calling. Not every woman wants children."

"It's true," I responded carefully, and with all of my own societal biases as a thirty-three-year-old woman who feels compelled into both marriage and motherhood. "But it takes a lot of courage not to live up to society's idea of what a woman should have in her life."

She nodded. "If only we could all be that brave," she said to me. "If only we could all choose not to live up to everyone else's expectations and do what feels right to us."

She still feels like she talks to God every single day, but she is quick to explain that she doesn't hear voices. She knows that would sound a little kooky.

"It is more that I get a sense of what God is saying to me." As she explained it to me, she looked past me and through a dusty window, at nothing but leaves and the shingles of the house next door.

"That is what keeps me going," she told me. "I try to pray in the morning, just sitting in the quiet of my room. I read the scripture of the day. I have a prayer list of people I pray for. When my mind is oblivious, when I am swimming, doing yoga, or driving, I catch myself talking to God. I usually say, 'Hey, I have this thing I am worried about getting done and I think I need some help here.'"

On most days, Sister Jeannine wakes in the morning delighted to go to work. Somehow she has managed to remain delighted in the face of serious oppression from within the Church. Working with the gay community has made her a target of the male bishops who would like to see her ministry eradicated completely. One particularly vociferous complaint came from Cardinal James Aloysius Hickey of Washington, DC.

Hickey was promoted to Archbishop of Washington, DC, by Pope John Paul II on June 17, 1980. On many issues he was liberal. He lobbied members of the US Congress to stop sending aid to the Contras in Nicaragua, and pushed his fellow bishops to take strong stands against increased military spending and in favor of nuclear disarmament. He was one of the first American bishops to address the issue of sexual abuse by clergy.

But on gay rights, Hickey remained conservative. In 1980 he began lodging formal complaints about New Ways Ministry with the Vatican. The Congregation for Institutes of Consecrated Life and Societies of Apostolic Life within the Holy See ordered both the Salvatorians, Fr. Bob Nugent's order of priests, and the School Sisters of Notre Dame to conduct three "internal studies" of the priest and the nun's activities.

Sister Jeannine's community had her back. Each time they got a letter, her fellow sisters responded to the Vatican that she was simply doing the work of the Church and recommended that she not be sanctioned. It was a more polite way of saying "Mind your own business."

Cardinal Hickey wouldn't be silenced so easily. He kept trying to convince the Vatican that what Sister Jeannine was doing was at odds with Church teachings and that it was dangerous. At one point he wrote to the Holy See:

"At the risk of trying your patience I write to you once again and ask that you bring pressure on Sister Jeannine's superiors to remove her from this ministry."

Cardinal Hickey's continued letters had their intended effect. In early 1988, the Vatican convened a three-member US-based committee headed by Bishop Adam Joseph Maida, the archbishop of Detroit, to render an official judgment on Sister Jeannine and Father Bob's gay ministry.

In May of 1988, the Congregation for the Doctrine of the Faith (CDF), then headed by Joseph Cardinal Ratzinger, who would later become Pope Benedict XVI, ordered the nun and the priest to sign a "Profession of Faith," declaring that they agreed with the Church's official stance on homosexuality. In 1999, the CDF released a report saying that the nun and the priest were prohibited from all forms of homosexual ministry.

Her community stood strong in support of her and her work, but they could not go against the Vatican's final decree. They asked that Sister Jeannine step away from the ministry. Father Bob was asked to do the same. He composed and signed his own "Profession of Faith" and separated himself from New Ways Ministry.

"We always knew if push came to shove what he would do and what I would do. But it was so hard for Bob," Sister Jeannine told me. "His priesthood was very important to him. There was no community of priests that would accept him."

She was torn. She didn't want to embarrass her community, and yet she felt bullied by these continued attacks on work that she knew made a major difference in people's lives every single day. She began a period of deep reflection, prayer, and retreat. "I still felt called to the ministry. I felt that what was being asked of me was unjust . . . that lesbian and gay people are so marginalized in the Church that they need an advocate. They need someone connected to the Church institution to speak on their behalf, and I felt that God was telling me, 'There is still work that you need to do here.'"

Her leaders in Notre Dame reluctantly told her that if she continued to work with the gay and lesbian community, they would need to dismiss her from their order. They were anguished. Sister Jeannine didn't want to cause them needless pain or to draw more of the Vatican's ire toward them, so she made the lateral move to the Sisters of Loretto, often referred to by conservative factions of the Catholic Church as an order of "feminist" nuns. In the nineteenth century, Loretto's founders, Mary Rhodes, Ann Havern, and Christina Stuart, started out teaching children on the Kentucky frontier. Maybe it was the frontier life that gave them a thicker skin than other orders. They were progressive visionaries on the frontier, and they remain on the front lines today.

I told Sister Jeannine that some people would be surprised to learn that the man, Fr. Bob Nugent, backed down in this situation and the woman was the one who held strong to her beliefs and wouldn't be bullied, wouldn't be submissive.

She sighed and nodded just slightly.

"The men are a little more cautious and fearful of the repercussions than the women. Women's communities are less afraid to take the risk," she said.

But joining a new order did nothing to divert the Vatican's interest. As Sister Jeannine made her transition to Loretto, the attacks from the patriarchy continued unabated.

A 2010 statement from the United States Conference of Catholic Bishops excoriated New Ways as an organization that "cannot legitimately speak for Catholics." Cardinal Francis George, OMI, archbishop of Chicago and president of the United States Conference of Catholic Bishops, issued the following statement about New Ways: "Their claim to be Catholic only confuses the faithful regarding the authentic teaching and ministry of the Church with respect to persons with a homosexual inclination. Accordingly, I wish to make it clear that, like other groups that claim to be Catholic but deny central aspects of Church teaching, New Ways Ministry has no approval or recognition from the Catholic Church and that they cannot speak on behalf of the Catholic faithful in the United States."

By 2009, the Loretto sisters had received nine letters from the Vatican informing them that if Sister Jeannine continued her ministry, she should leave their service voluntarily or be dismissed. Each time a letter was received, it was treated with respect and a response was sent, but the order had no plans to dismiss Sister Jeannine.

There is a button stuck on one of the bulletin boards in Sister Jeannine's house that reads: WE SHALL NOT BE SILENCED. I SUPPORT JEANNINE GRAMICK. She smiled as I looked at it.

"I don't like people to say I was silenced. The Vatican tried to silence me and it just didn't work."

This is a woman who, since the age of seven years old, has never wavered in her decision to be committed to Jesus Christ and has continually loved her Church. Regardless of everything she has gone through, Sister Jeannine still has a deep and abiding love and respect for the Church hierarchy because she believes they are the victims of an outdated theology that they feel bound to defend. Their sanctions against her make her feel ashamed for her Church's leaders.

"When the Vatican tries to silence people, it projects an image of Catholics to the world that I find embarrassing. I want to be proud of my Church and the bishops' actions just make me feel ashamed for them," Sister Jeannine told me. But there is also a selfish side to it. No one likes to be reprimanded.

"I don't like to be censured by a higher authority. I was always considered the good girl in school and in religious life. I don't like being in the position of the outcast, and that is how I felt then and how I still feel in many ways," she told me.

And yet in a small way, being an outcast of the Church hierarchy has helped Sister Jeannine relate even more to the people she serves.

"If you're a shepherd, you have to smell like the sheep, as Pope Francis says, and God knows I have now experienced just a tiny fraction of what gay and lesbian people have experienced their entire lives," she said.

As the battle for equality and gay marriage evolved at a rapid clip toward the end of President Barack Obama's first term, so too did Sister Jeannine's mission. It was no longer just about workshops and outreach; she believed that she was now needed on the front lines of the fight for gay marriage. She wanted to change the hearts and minds of Catholics across the country. She knew that this was a time and a place where she could truly make a difference.

In 2012, with a referendum on marriage equality on the

ballot in four states, Sister Jeannine traveled through Maryland, Maine, and Washington to speak to Catholics on the ground.

"We urged them to vote their conscience, because the bishops have a campaign against same-sex marriage which we believe is ill-advised," she said.

New Ways Ministry's official stance on the issue was as follows:

New Ways Ministry views the legalization of same-sex marriage as a matter of equal justice, not as a matter of sexual ethics. We believe it is important for the greater common good to protect the rights of couples in ALL adult, committed relationships based on the values of caring, compassion, love, mutuality, respect, and justice. Such Catholic values are more important than gender.

New Ways Ministry finds the notion that heterosexual marriage will be devalued and harmed if same-sex marriages are approved to be illogical and blind to empirical evidence. Problems with the traditional nuclear family as an institution began decades before the notion of same-sex marriage was raised as a political reality. Divorce rates among heterosexual couples skyrocketed many years before legislation to approve same-sex marriage was discussed. For centuries same-sex marriage has not been legal, and yet such a legal absence has had no positive effect on heterosexual marriages.

Instead of scapegoating same-sex marriage as causing the decline of the family and heterosexual unions, religious leaders should examine the economic, social, and cultural changes that have recently occurred to find the real causes of problems to these institutions. Only by finding the real causes will these leaders be able to start addressing real solutions.

We call on all Catholics to examine the social justice tradition of our Church—a tradition which values the freedom of conscience, the dignity of all human beings, and the protection of the common good—and to learn how these traditions have long been applied by Catholic leaders and thinkers to the protection of lesbian/gay people and their rights.

Sister Jeannine was in her element on the road. She gave what she calls "pep talks," miniature rallies wherein she told crowds of Catholics that it was completely OK in the eyes of God for them to vote in favor of gay marriage. The fight for equality, she argued, is not about sacramental marriage, but legal marriage.

"We didn't get the backlash from the Catholics on the ground. We had mostly support from them," she said. She began a campaign to collect signatures of Catholics who would publicly say that they would vote for marriage equality.

"There is nothing in the Gospel against gay marriage

and homosexuality. We need to take into account the science, psychology, and justice, of course," was the message Sister Jeannine stuck to when addressing the skeptics. Voters in Maryland assured Sister Jeannine that she had influenced them to vote their conscience. "It was a good sign that we are growing up as a Church. Half of Catholics are in favor of gay marriage," she said. "In a way, it is nice to start growing obsolete. We're finding so many Catholics on board with lesbian and gay issues that they don't need us anymore," she said half-jokingly. A 2011 survey by the Public Religion Institute showed that 52 percent of Catholics believe that same-sex couples should indeed be allowed to marry.

Outcry from the patriarchy aside, the shifting sentiment in favor of equality for gays and lesbians among average Catholics gives Sister Jeannine a certain sense of vindication for the issue she has championed for most of her life. From that moment when she met Dominic in that row house in West Philadelphia, she knew that with time, prayer, and hard work, what was rotten in the Catholic Church could be made new. The fact that Catholics came out in favor of gay marriage forty years after she held her ministry for that group of gay men gave her hope that even more positive change could be possible in the Church.

"In my day and age, growing up in the Catholic ghetto, we Catholics were not trained to be thinkers," she told me. "We were trained to do what the religious authority suggested. I don't mean to say that we shouldn't have religious authorities, but we need authorities who will give guidance and direction. If we want to grow in our own moral lives, then we need to make our own decisions, not merely follow the decision that someone else makes for us."

The congregations have come around, but the fight that remains is with the old men of the Church. "Now we need to work on the American bishops," Sister Jeannine told me. In November of 2013, before a mostly full Cathedral of the Immaculate Conception in Springfield, Illinois, Bishop Thomas John Paprocki, wearing a royal-purple robe, staged an "exorcism," asking God to deliver the world from the evil of same-sex marriage just as Illinois governor Pat Quinn was signing the state's gay marriage bill into law.

Sister Jeannine has met with Bishop Paprocki, and they have had a debate about same-sex marriage.

"We were on completely opposite sides," she told me. "But as a person, he is a good person, and we have had an e-mail correspondence. That is what Francis wants us to do. He wants us to get to know the bishops and talk to each other. He wants a dialogue."

Despite everything the Vatican has done to thwart her mission, Sister Jeannine is optimistic about Pope Francis.

"I am so much more hopeful now than I was with Pope Benedict. If we had more Pope Francises at the lower level, then we could have the Church that we want," she told me, her bright-blue eyes growing wide with anticipation and her apple-round cheeks flushing with excitement. She quotes Francis with regularity, waving her hands in the air like an orchestra conductor punctuating his words with a crescendo. Her line about smelling like the sheep came from a March 2013 Mass the new pope gave in St. Peter's Basilica, where he urged the priests to live with the people most in need. "Be shepherds with the smell of sheep," the new pope advised. "So that people can sense the priest is not just concerned with his own congregation, but is also a fisher of men." On a July morning, the pope was returning from his first papal trip abroad from World Youth Day in Brazil. He was unusually candid in answering a slew of reporter questions, including one on the issue of gay priests in the Vatican.

"We shouldn't marginalize people for this. They must be integrated into society," Pope Francis said. "If someone is gay and he searches for the Lord and has good will, who am I to judge?"

It was a change in tone to be sure, but the pope gave no indication that he was ready to modify the doctrine that views homosexuality as intrinsically disordered. Still, it was a giant step past his predecessors. Sister Jeannine believes that with prodding and education Francis may just see things the New Ways way.

"You know what I think Francis's problem is, Jo?" Sister Jeannine asked me, licking jam off her fingers as she cleared our plates away and packed some scones in a Tupperware container for me to take on the train back to New York.

"What, Jeannine?" I replied, prepared for a doctrinal assessment.

"I just don't think he has met enough assertive women in his life."

4.

Racing Against Time, Outliving the Competition

Heading to the finish line of the Ironman is like me getting to the pearly gates. I think that is why I smile every time at the finish.

—Sister Madonna Buder

She'd made a wager with God. If she couldn't complete the 2012 Canadian Ironman triathlon, Sister Madonna Buder wouldn't attempt this insane race ever again. The nun was exhausted and beaten down as she dove into the silvery blue water of Lake Okanagan. She just didn't want to put herself through the pain and the agony, the torn ligaments and the broken ribs, any longer. Still, for this one race, possibly her last race, she willed her muscles to make another stroke, which they did as her limbs trembled like twigs laden down with ice.

The race was actually going surprisingly well at every turn. Sister Madonna was able to ward off her usual stomach issues much longer than usual. She made it eight miles to the finish line before finally, as she likes to describe it in the sweetest voice you can imagine talking about such things, "giving up my cookies."

She doesn't wear a watch when she races (can't see it in the dark anyway, she says), but by the time she was in the home stretch, finishing the marathon portion of the race along Lakeshore Drive, Sister Madonna knew that God had won the bet. Adrenaline coursed through her veins and with crowds roaring her name she crossed the finish line in sixteen hours and thirty-six minutes—twenty-four minutes shy of the seventeen-hour cutoff to officially complete the Ironman.

"Ladies and gentlemen, we now have a world record!" the announcer Steve King boomed over a loudspeaker at the finish line with his signature game-show-host enthusiasm on August 26, 2012. At age eighty-two, Sister Madonna Buder was the oldest athlete, male or female, to ever successfully complete an Ironman triathlon. God had bested her. Sister Madonna would go on to race another day.

Sister Madonna's nicknames include "The Mother Superior of Triathlon" and "The Iron Nun," both in honor of the more than 366 triathlons she's done, forty-six of which were Ironman distances, since taking up running at age forty-seven. She has this real no-nonsense attitude about the whole thing and is always asking what the big fuss is about. "Why do people care about this little old lady running these races?" she says. As she sees it, God gave her this body that happens to be good at running incredibly long distances. Why shouldn't she use it?

Looking at Sister Madonna, you can't help but think that body was made for racing and little else. Her petite 5'7", 115-pound frame carries nothing more than what it needs to propel her over miles of road. She is all sinewy muscle over tanned arms and legs. Her cerulean-blue eyes sparkle teasingly beneath an adorable pageboy of brown hair with just a sprinkling of gray.

As for the pain? It's just an annoying by-product. In the course of the more than three decades that Sister Madonna has competed in races, her delicate body has been battered, bruised, and broken.

"I'm like a Dresden doll. I think I have broken almost every part of me that can be broken," Sister Madonna told me, comparing herself to a china toy. In all, she has flown over the handlebars of a bicycle more times than any liv-ing human has the right to. She's broken her ribs countless times, her right hip in two places, her right arm six times, her left arm twice, and let's not mention her shoulder, clav-icle, and nearly all her fingers and toes.

When she competes, she looks just like everyone else in the race, wearing brightly colored running tights. The only giveaway that she may be something a little apart from the crowd is the silver cross hanging from her neck.

Her yearly competition schedule can include more than twenty races. She has dialed it back since turning eighty, but not by much. She often travels alone, leaning on the Lord to be her travel agent.

"I trust that once I get my foot out the door, God will pro-vide the rest, even where I rest my head," Sister Madonna told me. "Relying on Him has always helped with finding a place to stay—whether it is a tent, on someone's sofa, or bedding down in my own car." Once, she was forced to spend the night in the Greensboro, North Carolina, air-port after a connecting flight was abruptly canceled. Sister Madonna hardly thought it would be worth it to leave the airport and pay for a place to stay for just a few hours. One of the entry gates was under construction, so she poked around until she found somewhere suitable and then just slept on a wooden pallet that was covered in plastic bubble wrap. She narrowly avoided being hauled off to jail and spent the night hearing a *pop-pop-pop* every time she rolled left or right. Another time, during the 1998 ITU World Championship Triathlon in Lausanne, she was taken to a Swiss hospital for hyperthermia and an asthma attack immediately after she finished. When she was discharged from the hospital, she had on nothing more than her race attire and no money, but found her way to a bus that could return her to the race site.

She is her own Sherpa, hauling her bike everywhere she goes, breaking it down and putting it back together like a grease monkey before and after each race. The amount of travel to make it to twenty-five-odd races around the globe in a year is exhausting enough for anyone, let alone a woman in her eighties. In the spring of 2012, she hop-scotched across seven different states in an eight-week period.

The Iron Nun was born Dorothy Marie Buder in St. Louis, Missouri, on a day in 1930 she says was "hotter than hell." Her mother insisted everyone call her by both her first and middle names. She wouldn't become Madonna until the day she took her final vows.

Sister Madonna inherited her athleticism from her father and her faith from her mother. Gustavus A. Buder Jr. was a championship oarsman in St. Louis and an analytical Unitarian who wasn't expecting to fall madly in love with a French Catholic budding actress, but that was exactly what he got in Kathryn, who charmed him with her portrayal of a female Shylock in a production of Shakespeare's

The Merchant of Venice. Interfaith marriages were a rarity at the beginning of the twentieth century, but Gustavus, a civil rights lawyer, full of integrity and persistence, found a priest who was willing to intercede. Kathryn baptized her first child and only daughter in the hospital herself and then taught her the catechism at home.

As a baby, Madonna was active from the get-go. In one home movie, she looks like she may be doing push-ups in her crib. One of Sister Madonna's favorite photos from childhood features her running wildly, curls flailing in the air, little white dress catching air behind her, as she scurries away from a nurse into her father's arms. In her later years, her long runs would remind her of that child. She was a beautiful tomboy who always preferred doing anything outdoors to staying inside. She became adept at sailing, horseback riding, hiking, and mountain climbing.

When she was ten, her father finally relented and allowed Madonna and her brother to be properly baptized at the Saint Louis University College Church.

The pair went out to play afterward. Madonna felt light and giddy as she rode the playground swings, tilting her face skyward to drink in the heavenly rays of the sun. When another little girl asked her how it felt to be baptized, she replied, "I am a child of God now." She was high on spirituality. Her brother, in turn, said he felt nothing.

That was the first time Sister Madonna felt particularly called by God. She told me that she knew from age fourteen that she wanted to be a nun, but her mother thought it was important for her to try out all of the normal things girls her age did, including dating. Her parents had yet to explain anything about the facts of life. After one coed party in the sixth grade, Madonna came home and told her parents about a game they had played involving a spinning milk bottle and a kiss. Her parents were nonplussed. On another evening she told them about a game the kids were playing in Forest Park called Snipe, which was the opposite of hide-and-seek. Instead of losing, the first person to be found received a kiss.

"My parents heard the word 'kiss' once too often and they decided the solution was, rather than explain the birds and the bees to me, to transfer me to an all-girls school," Sister Madonna said. She called Visitation Academy "The Dungeon" since it was a huge castle replete with gargoyles, a belfry, and long dark corridors.

The sisters at Visitation Academy had an immediate effect on the young girl, especially her grammar teacher, Sister Consolata, who was unendingly patient with Madonna as she struggled to learn how to diagram sentences. Sister Madonna describes in her autobiography, *The Grace to Race*, how she was influenced by the nuns and would watch them from the corners of the chapel as they chanted at Vespers each afternoon before her study hall. Back at home, Madonna built a small altar to the Virgin Mary in her bedroom, where she would sit in her free time meditating and praying. From the start, she felt a special bond with the Blessed Mother.

Being pretty and popular, Madonna was courted by many eligible young men, including the late Dr. Tom Dooley, who was a dynamo at the piano. An accomplished equestrian, she appeared on the cover of *Tempo* magazine in 1951 looking like the spitting image of Elizabeth Taylor at the same age. Her dance card was always completely full.

Even with all this attention, she felt a distinct emptiness and knew something was missing in her life.

"It was then I knew that no man was going to be able to fill the recesses of my heart like God Himself," Sister Madonna told me. The hardest thing about knowing she would become a nun was breaking the news to her father. Though she invited him to lunch one day in public to announce it, this did not restrain his tears, as he had expected her to tell him she was engaged to the young Irish Marine she had been spending so much time with, so well had she held the secret in her heart.

Once in the convent, the elder sisters usually ask the young nuns what their choice of name will be after they take their final vows. But to her dismay, no one ever asked her. She dropped hints like crazy, but to no avail. However, she couldn't have been happier when they bestowed the name Sister Madonna on her.

Two profound events changed everything in Sister

Madonna's life. The first was the day in December 1956 when she professed her final vows to the Sisters of the Good Shepherd. She would spend the next twenty-odd years in God's service working with socially disadvantaged young girls committed by the courts and receiving two master's degrees, one in education and the other in counseling, from Arizona State University.

Then came her second moment of conversion, the day that she took her first run. She began running just a few weeks shy of her forty-eighth birthday at the suggestion of Fr. John Topel, a Jesuit priest who was conducting a workshop on spirituality at Rockaway on the Oregon coast. The priest thought running would be a joyful release for her, harmonizing mind, body, and soul, producing a sense of relaxation, calmness, and intimacy with the Almighty.

"Nothing could be that good," Sister Madonna defiantly told him. Father John liked her spirit and dared her to run out on the beach in between two eddies without getting wet. Never one to back down from a challenge, she found a pair of running shorts in a pile of donation clothes and dug a pair of secondhand sneakers, given to her by her sister-in-law, out of her bag. To her surprise, the priest was right. The running felt good. She ran for five minutes without stopping, parallel to the slate-gray waves at dusk, her feet sinking into the sand in a soft crescendo, in between the two eddies half a mile apart. Father John was impressed.

"You must keep it up now," he said. Sister Madonna ran along the beach every day for the remainder of the retreat. When she returned to the Sisters of the Good Shepherd convent in Spokane, Washington, she ran around the girls' ballfield, guessing that twenty-eight laps was about seven miles. She wore long pants that flapped at the ankles and the same secondhand sneakers with thin flat soles to train for her first race, the local Bloomsday race of 8.2 miles, just five weeks after she began running.

She was harder on her body than she had ever been in her entire life, her calves becoming tight and her knees so swollen that she could hardly bend them. By her third week of training for Bloomsday, she broke down in tears.

She cried to God, "I just can't do it." When she quieted down, she heard what she describes as this small inner voice respond, "I know you're stepping out in faith, not knowing what the end results will be, but I too had to step out in faith, complying with my Father's will, not knowing how many people down through the ages would respond to my supreme act of love by laying down my life for them." Then she pulled herself together and stepped out the side door for another excruciating run.

God is always with Sister Madonna. Their relationship isn't about Him being "up there" and her being "down here." She has intimate conversations in her head with God all day long. She prays when she runs, calling the movement a type of prayer posture. Sometimes she prays for individuals, as in her first-ever Bloomsday race when she prayed to God to transfer her will to endure to her brother to help him overcome his alcoholism and try to save the marriage that the disease was destroying. The marriage eventually broke apart, but his second wife was a Baptist who kept him from drinking, so Sister Madonna believes her prayers were answered in the end. On her long runs she sometimes recites the repetitive Hail Marys of the Rosary to lose track of the miles.

"Running not only helped me solve my problems, it reduced my anxiety and cleared my soul, taking away any brooding darkness that took away my positive attitude," she told me.

Sometimes she is less specific with her prayers, just allowing herself to meditate on her surroundings, God's creation, and the feeling of wholeness and balance she experiences as her feet fall on the pavement. These meditations often take the form of haikus she composes about nature. She repeats the lines of the poems in her head over and over until she can get home to write them down.

Songs of bird waking
Introducing a new day
Sweetly soothe the soul

Stillness, then movement
Sudden breeze comes from nowhere
Stirring emotions

*   *   *

When she has trouble breathing, she will wheeze the Lord's name in and out—Jesus on the inhale and Jesus on the exhale. This hallowed breathing has sustained her for hours at a time.

"When nothing is happening and people pop into my mind for no good reason, I just ask the Lord to bless them then and there because I figure they probably need prayers," she said.

During one race, Sister Madonna was praying in her head, *Bless the Lord.* One foot dropped. *Praise His Holy Name.* Down went the other. She noticed a man in the road who was struggling and didn't look like he could make it any farther. She began chanting the prayer out loud. When she reached him, she called out to him. "Try it! It will help pick up your pace!" she yelled into the wind. He mustered his strength and began the chant, racing ahead of her, but he waited for her at the finish line. They crossed together and finished the prayer. He wrote the words on the back of his race jersey so he would remember her. It is instances like this that make Sister Madonna a staple at races, the unofficial chaplain of the racing world. Race officials often ask her to do invocations at the starting line, and on more than one occasion she has helped to pray away bad weather, including a hurricane that once threatened a race.

Sometimes people will linger alongside her and ask

quietly if they can just touch her for good luck. "So many people see her as an inspiration," Ironman announcer Steve King told me. "The aura around her is stunning, whether you are religious or not. People just melt in her presence."

Learning to run in her late forties helped Sister Madonna rediscover the adventurous spirit she had been missing since she entered the convent. She wanted to push herself further, and as she approached age fifty, she wanted a new adventure. A year earlier she was sitting at home spending a rare night in front of the television when she spotted a movie starring Joanne Woodward called *See How She Runs.* In the movie, a middle-aged schoolteacher struggles to complete the Boston Marathon. Sister Madonna was taken by the character's persistence in the race. The agony Ms. Woodward's character experienced in that film reminded her of the many agonies endured by Christ as he was carrying the cross to Calvary.

"In one scene in the movie, someone hands her a towel to wipe the sweat from her face. I thought immediately of Veronica using her veil to wipe the bloody sweat from Jesus's face while he was carrying the cross," Sister Madonna told me.

And so, shortly after the Bloomsday race, Sister Madonna knew that she wanted to run a marathon, choosing to take

JO PIAZZA

on the race in Boston that she had seen in the film. The decision made her order nervous. What would people think? Their little Bloomsday race was one thing, but a nun in shorts, running in front of thousands of people in a big city, with millions watching at home? That would be a spectacle. Would people laugh at her? What would the priests think? What if the Vatican found out?

One of her fellow sisters even commented, "You are such a free spirit. We don't know how to contain you." Sister Madonna restrained herself, but inside she was thinking, Why should you try to?

This was 1982, twenty years after the start of the Second Vatican Council. By then, plenty of sisters had already given up their long-skirted black habits. In 1966, one avant-garde order, the Daughters of Charity, even consulted the French fashion designer Christian Dior about what they should wear in the habit's stead. Dior created a new modern habit with sleek, angular lines that showed slightly more skin. But Sister Madonna's order wasn't so progressive. They were one of the few clinging tightly to the old ways and still wore a modified habit well into the early 1980s. That was just fine with Sister Madonna, who preferred conservative dress anyway. Even today, she wishes orders hadn't been so quick to give it up and still longs for the days when even laywomen wore long ballerina-style skirts instead of pants, asserting, "It is a rarity to see women in skirts anymore."

Some of the sisters suggested she wear the habit while

she ran. When Sister Madonna pictured herself on the starting line of a race in full habit, she knew that would be even more of a spectacle; by wearing shorts, she would melt into the scenery. All she wanted out of this important race was to be lost in the crowd. She didn't even know if she would be able to finish it, so there was definitely no need to call even more attention to herself. She would wear the shorts!

Times may have changed, but Sister Madonna didn't want to blindside anyone with her plans. She figured it would be best to alert the local bishop that she would be participating. She was nervous when she saw him sitting stern and upright in his chair as she approached.

"Bishop, I want to tell you about a plan I have to run the Boston Marathon, taking pledges for MS, a cause greater than myself," Sister Madonna said in the biggest voice she could muster. He visibly relaxed and his lips curled into a grin as he gave her his blessing. As she was leaving, he called out to her, "I wish some of my priests would do what you are doing."

Sister Madonna called on Jesus for help during the last four miles of the Boston Marathon. Not stopping at any aid stations along the race course, she began to struggle during the final four miles of the race. Her prayer pulled her through. Wearing the T-shirt the sisters had given her before her departure with a paraphrase from Saint Paul (Philippians

3:4) that read RUNNING TOWARD THE GOAL, she completed twenty-six miles with a time of three hours and thirty-eight minutes. She was fifty-two. The next year, she shaved six minutes off her time. As of 2013, she has run the Boston Marathon seven more times.

Sister Madonna believes that whatever talent she has is God-given, and He obviously expects her to use it. The words of Christ continue to inspire her: "You have not chosen me. I have chosen you" (John 15:16). She had not chosen to run. Running had been introduced to her by a priest. A triathlon was the next obvious step for the nun.

She recalls thinking, "Well, I've done the epitome of foolishness by engaging in the marathon at my age; why not try this thing too?" She was perfectly capable on a bicycle, though she hadn't actually ridden one in years, and that was her mother's balloon-tired cruiser bike with no handbrakes—you just reverse-pedaled to halt it. As a kid, she would swim in Lake Michigan on family vacations, but she was terrified of the idea of swimming in a swarming school of flailing limbs. She tried to ignore these apprehensions as she prepared for the challenge.

Her first triathlon was a local race in Spokane called Heels & Wheels, where the three-quarter-mile swim took place in a local pool and the twelve-mile biking section rolled up and down lush green hills. Her second race was the Troika, a formidable half Ironman of 1.2 miles of swimming, 56 miles of biking, and 13.1 miles of running. Her competitive edge was getting sharper, and she began to understand how people could become addicted to the highs of distance running. Throughout her first ten years of racing, she struggled to remain true to herself and not let her competitive streak push her beyond what seemed reasonable. "Know Thyself" and "To Thine Own Self Be True" became her new mantras. There weren't triathlon coaches around in the late '80s, so Sister Madonna just winged it. Even though she was able to curb her own competitive spirit, she couldn't control that in others. You might think no one would bully an elderly nun, but you would be wrong! During a triathlon on the Gold Coast in Australia, a woman in Sister Madonna's age group tried to psych her out.

"I understand they have sharks out there," the woman said before the pair plunged into the salty sea. Sister Madonna simply smiled sweetly back and said, "Oh, those poor things! How will they know which of these thrashing bodies to choose? They'll probably be freaked out." It was the perfect response, and after that the woman didn't torment her anymore. Sister Madonna beat her in that race.

It was only a matter of time before momentum propelled Sister Madonna into an Ironman. She had just celebrated her silver anniversary, twenty-five years with the Sisters of the Good Shepherd, when her friend Roy Allen, a retired police officer and fellow triathlete, returned from his first successful Ironman in Kona, Hawaii.

"Sister, you have got to do this race," Allen said, still high from completing his first Ironman. He had piqued her curiosity and she couldn't let go of the challenge, but as usual, God had other plans. While training, various accidents kept delaying her entry into the Ironman race at Kona. While visiting St. Louis for her parents' fifty-fifth wedding anniversary, Sister Madonna borrowed her nephew's bike for a ride around town. Suicide brakes, so named because they stop one abruptly, were a new concept to the nun, and upon squeezing them the way she would other brakes, she flew over the handlebars.

"I had no idea I was gushing blood from my elbow," Sister Madonna said. It turned out to be a compound fracture that would keep her in the hospital for a week. Afraid her legs would atrophy while she was bedridden, she snuck into the stairwell at night to run up and down the eight flights of stairs. Three weeks later, she ran the Diet Pepsi Championship 10K race in New York City in a half-cast, taking fourth place among the women in her age group. She planned to take on the Ironman again the next year, but yet another borrowed bike interfered with her well-laid plans.

On September 8, 1984, just a month before the Hawaiian Ironman, Sister Madonna biked out to Liberty Lake on the Washington–Idaho border to take in an open-water swim. On the ride back, she was crossing traffic with the green light when a car came directly at her from behind. She swerved and cleared the car by four inches, falling down hard on her left hip. It was broken in two places.

"I knew this Ironman attempt was also a goner," she told me. "I thought, *God, what do you think about me doing an Ironman, anyway?*" She later realized that the accident precipitated a major turning point in her life.

"Having to lay with my leg raised above my heart to prevent any further advance of phlebitis originating from the broken hip, one of our sisters thrust a book into my hands called *Sudden Spring,* written by Lillanna Kopp—formerly a Holy Name sister," Sister Madonna told me. It described a new concept of religious life suggested by Pope John XXIII during the Second Vatican Council that led to the founding of Sisters for Christian Community, a group of religious women that called for a more participatory vocation in which all women were considered coequals.

"In keeping with the times, it seemed a perfect fit for me," Sister Madonna went on. "I took my vows at their annual assembly in St. Louis, my own hometown, that year. These sisters have continued to be a source of encouragement and inspiration to me."

By the following year, Sister Madonna was finally healed and able to compete.

The woman taking the entries at Kona squinted at the nun through sun-crinkled eyes with a look of serious concern. She told the little old nun she didn't think she could handle the high temperatures during the Hawaiian race.

But Sister Madonna responded, "Really, I can take the heat. I was born in a hundred and five degrees in St. Louis and have been used to the heat ever since."

She was still limping from the hip injury, and to make matters worse, a few months earlier she had fallen again and broken some ribs while continuing to train after completing a marathon in Australia. When she reached Hawaii, cortisone shots dulled some of the pain, but a new obstacle loomed: a hurricane was expected to hit the Big Island the day of the big race. Instead, it veered out into the ocean, whipping up the currents with four-foot swells.

A man on a surfboard kept paddling next to Sister Madonna after the swim turnaround, yelling instructions, but as she neared the pier, she felt like she was swimming in place. The scenery below her never changed. As a result, she was four minutes shy of the two-hour-and-fifteen-minute cutoff, which prevented her from taking off on the bike. Her first Ironman was doomed. Had the cutoff been the usual two hours and twenty minutes, as it is today, she would have made it.

"Yet I was so close, I just kept thinking to myself that I had to do it again. Nothing is impossible with God," she said.

The next year, 1986, she completed the race in fourteen hours and thirty-one minutes, despite stopping during the running portion to help a dehydrated woman and walking with her until an ambulance came.

Since then, Sister Madonna has competed in one or two

Ironman competitions a year, in addition to a handful of half Ironman distances, triathlons of other lengths, and running events including marathons. Sister Madonna's best-ever Ironman time came at age sixty-two, when she finished in thirteen hours and sixteen minutes.

She giggles when people ask her how she trains.

"I don't. I really don't. I like to tell them I just keep moving all the time. I run to church when I can. I literally *run* errands," Sister Madonna said. "I watch for chances to bike outdoors whenever I can. I really don't enjoy using mechanical devices indoors."

She doesn't have a coach, at least not in the physical sense of the word.

"My coach is the Man Upstairs," she says. "He gave me a body to listen to. I don't need any contraptions to listen to my body. It speaks out loud enough."

She actually takes the shortest route possible in her runs from the small mobile home she lives in all by herself to Mass at St. Anthony's Church in Spokane, Washington, most days, making the round trip of just under five miles in long pants that are suitably conservative for a Catholic Mass. She rides or runs almost everywhere, some days doing a mini-triathlon just to get around, which requires squeezing in a mile-plus swim as well. She lives by the sun's cycle, going to bed when it is dark, waking up when it is light, never setting an alarm. She eats what is available, mostly carbohydrates and fresh vegetables and fruits. She grows what she can in a small garden and occasionally indulges in her weakness for chocolate-chip cookies. In the summer she laps up ice cream almost every single day.

"You can't give up ice cream," she told me. "I have done nothing knowledgeable to pollute my body, but alcohol and caffeine are acceptable for enjoyment's sake."

Her roughshod training regimen employs the following guidelines: don't waste time training when you can incorporate it into your daily routine, thus making workouts a part of your daily lifestyle; try to make it as joyful as possible to avoid burnout; vary your routine to avoid boredom. Training indoors gives her no joy, as she told me, so she rarely does it, unless inclement weather gives her no choice.

When the cold comes to Spokane, the kind of damp cold that nestles in and camps out in your bones for four months, she hardly trains at all.

"I dislike sitting on a piece of training equipment watching those digital numbers turn around. It's always so hard to see the warmth and sun go," she lamented when I spoke to her over the phone on the first truly cold day in Washington. Sister Madonna has a difficult time saying anything negative about nature, so she is quick to tack on an addendum: "But if I didn't have the change of seasons, I wouldn't be able to hibernate like God's lesser creatures."

It has been tricky to set up phone calls with Sister Madonna, as technology is peripheral to her life. She has neither cell phone nor computer, but she knows every spot in town that has Internet access. When she needs to use the Internet, she will bike or run to those locations. Whenever we arranged for a phone conversation, we had to pack in as much talking as possible or I would miss her for another week.

During one of our talks, we got on the topic of her motivation. She is adamant that she races on God's command. When she wants to drag her heels, He pushes her forward. She races for those who seem inspired by what she does.

"They want to see this age group expanding and expanding," she said. "I don't understand why I mean so much to them, but it doesn't matter. I don't have to understand. If they want or need a carrot on a string, I am willing to be that for them."

She takes issue with those who might criticize her. "Who says I can't be in the Church and doing God's work everywhere I go?" she has said. "There is no limit, no boundaries, to when and where you can commune with God. It doesn't have to be in church all the time. It's not me. It's about what God does in and through us."

Neglecting her talents would actually be an insult to God, she tells me. "If He gives you a talent, He expects you to use it. Not to do it would just insult His generosity."

When Sister Madonna was in her fifties, she was the

only fifty-year-old woman doing marathons. Then that division began to slowly fill up. She has opened five age group divisions for women since then: 60–64, 65–69, 70–74, 75–79, and then 80-plus. So far, she is her only competition in her age group.

"I am racing against time," she says. "But I am also outliving the competition. It would be awfully nice to open up the race for women in their nineties."

5.

An Underground Railroad for Modern-Day Slaves

*To say a person has been trafficked is to say they have
had their freedom taken away from them through force, fraud,
or coercion. They are treated like a commodity, not a person, and
their humanity is stripped away from them.*

—Sister Joan Dawber

What had I done?

I covered my eyes with my hands and splayed them apart just an inch to see a nineteen-year-old Asian woman on the movie screen in front of me handcuffed and whipped by a dominatrix while her pimp looked on menacingly, smoking crystal meth out of a dirty pipe.

Sitting next to me was an unfailingly proper British nun in her sixties, my guest at this film premiere of a movie called *Eden*, which tells the story of a Korean American girl sold into sex slavery.

With each increasingly sexualized scene (a male sexual organ is bitten off in the middle of the film), I became more convinced that I'd made the same kind of mistake I had made when I watched *Brokeback Mountain* with my conservative father.

"We can leave," I whispered during a particularly disturbing scene.

Sister Joan Dawber just shook her head a little.

"I may close my eyes if this gets to be too bad," she replied, as calm as ever. I was the one shielding my face for most of the movie.

I was surprised when Sister Joan took me up on my offer to see *Eden*. I forwarded her the invite only moments after it arrived in my inbox, not really expecting a response, just thinking it could be the kind of thing she would be interested in, wanting to be friendly. I had actually forgotten that I had even sent it until she wrote back to me three days later:

Thanks for this very kind invitation, Jo. Yes, I am planning to join you, however, I have a meeting from 5:15–6:15 in Queens then I will drive into the city. Let me know where we should meet. Thanks.

She was waiting for me when I arrived and wrapped me in a warm hug in front of the Film Forum on a dimly lit block of West Houston Street in Manhattan, about thirteen miles from her home in Queens.

"I can't believe I drove in here so late, look at me!" she said, spreading her arms wide and looking up at the slightly shabby neon-blue marquee. "So this is where the artsy people all hang out." Sure enough, a group of black-turtle-necked, dark-rimmed-glasses-wearing hipsters elbowed past us through the glass doors, knocking Sister Joan into me. She just laughed and grabbed my arm as we walked into the theater.

Thirty minutes later, I was nervously checking that Sister Joan was all right. I didn't need to be nervous. As the executive director of the LifeWay Network, running one of only three safe houses in New York City for women survivors of human trafficking, she hears stories worse than the ones portrayed in *Eden* every single day.

She has a dangerous job.

The location of the house is kept secret from everyone but a select few other nuns and volunteers who help Sister Joan with the house operations. If its location were made known, the lives of the sisters who run it and the women they are trying to protect would be in jeopardy. The majority of the people, mostly men, who traffic the women are still at large, and Sister Joan is essentially stealing from their bank accounts by harboring their chattel.

In nun circles, word of mouth travels fast, so I had heard

133

stories about Sister Joan well before I met her. One afternoon, I was taking the Staten Island Ferry with Sister Simone Campbell and the rest of the "Nuns on the Bus." As the crowd of sisters, most with short gray hair and sensible wash-and-wear outfits, power-walked their way commandingly through Whitehall Station to board the boat across the New York Harbor, I explained this book project to them.

"It's about how badass nuns are. You know, all of the great work you guys all do," I explained, giving my elevator pitch. They began buzzing among themselves, many of them having the same thought at the same time.

"You have to meet Joan Dawber," one sister with a particularly gravelly voice told me. "She rescues sex slaves . . . has a safe house for them." Soon everyone within earshot agreed that I had to meet her, and I was provided with three different ways in which to contact her. That is how things with nuns usually happen. They are quick to come to a consensus and convince you their consensus is the *exact* course of action needed in order to find an elegant solution to a problem. If nuns ran the world, things would just get done. No questions asked.

I set about convincing Sister Joan to meet with me. After months of e-mailing with Arlene, Sister Joan's watchdog of an administrative assistant, we met for the first time just a couple of weeks before going to see *Eden*. In person, Sister Joan is the last woman you would expect to be running a dangerous modern-day Underground Railroad. Her voice has a melodic singsong like Julie Andrews's Maria in *The Sound of Music,* which can immediately put anyone at ease. She is slight and quick in movement. Her face is unlined and quite beautiful. She wore a heather-gray cardigan, nearly the same color as her short but stylish hair that just brushed her earlobes, the sweater drowning her birdlike wrists. New York City had been overwhelmed with a small blizzard that week and I arrived on her doorstep in Forest Hills, Queens, covered in ice and snow, my socks soaked through to my feet and makeup dripping down my face.

"Oh, I didn't think you would actually make it here," Sister Joan fussed as she let me in the door. I had expected someone bigger, maybe burlier, someone who could take down the kinds of men who hold women in captivity. I marveled at little Sister Joan.

She busied herself with taking my coat and scarf and getting me settled into a chair next to her desk so she could tell me her story.

Back in 2001, a group of six hundred female congregation leaders from around the world, known as the Union of Superiors General, met in Rome for a conference to discuss the issues they believed nuns should be tackling in the twenty-first century. One contingent of sisters from Africa was very vocal about the need for sisters to address the growing global problem of human trafficking.

That inspired the congregational leader of Sister Joan's order to send out a letter asking her sisters to take a closer look at the issue. When Sister Joan took it to heart, her Mother Superior joked that Sister Joan was the only one who ever bothered to read her letter.

"When I read about it, I felt squeamish," Sister Joan said. "It was a world I didn't want to get to know." She didn't want to fall down the rabbit hole of something so "wounded and violent and stripped of hope." But she felt called to pray on it.

"I didn't even want to look at it because it was too upsetting," she said. "I thought I would just pray about it . . . but of course, when we pray, it isn't the other people who are changed, it is us who get changed, and as I prayed I got stronger. I knew there was a desire in me to assist. I can't explain it any better than to just say that it became clear to me. I had a sense that I could make a difference."

In 2005, at a conference on human trafficking in Baltimore run by the Migration and Refugee Services branch of the United States Conference of Catholic Bishops, Sister Joan found a group of like-minded religious folks who wanted to tackle the issue with her. It was God's divine providence that had brought them all together in the same place, she told me. The seven sisters at the conference hailed from five different congregations in New York. During their meeting they decided to form a coalition and met later that year at the motherhouse for the Sisters of Charity of New York on September 28, 2005. Sister Mary Heyser, RSHM, chaired the meeting and became the glue for the group that would be known as NY-CRC-STOP: New York Coalition of Religious Congregations to Stop Trafficking of People.

Human trafficking is defined by the US State Department as "activities involved when one person obtains or holds another person in compelled service." International, national, and state laws provide varying definitions, typically emphasizing the exploitation of another human being. To Sister Joan, human trafficking is no less than modern-day slavery.

"If you think about how individuals were taken against their will, used as commodities, and sold as commodities, that is what is happening today in the experience of human trafficking. Individuals are tricked through all kinds of ploys. Unlike slavery in the past, it isn't along racial lines. It is among the vulnerable population."

After those first meetings with like-minded religious folks, Sister Joan racked her brain thinking about how she could provide something of actual value to the victims.

The key, she believed, was safe housing. These women couldn't do anything until they had a safe place to live. She asked her order if she could give up her full-time work in parish ministry to work on the trafficking issue on a more regular basis. When they agreed, she started her research full-time.

"Joan and I tried to visit places with safe houses so we could get a feel for the setup and meet women who were living there," Sister Mary Heyser explained.

Like a holier version of Thelma and Louise, the pair hit the road together, traveling across the country to California to see one of the only safe houses in America specifically designated for the safe housing of women. There, the Coalition to Abolish Slavery & Trafficking welcomed the sisters and gave them a tour of their grounds.

"We were actually really honored to be able to do that. They didn't do that for other people," Sister Joan said.

Standing in the garden after they'd walked through the house and met the women staying there, Sister Joan met Sister Mary's gaze. Both women knew there was no turning back.

"I said, 'Mary, we are really going to do this,'" Sister Joan recalled to me, mustering that same fresh determination and sitting up straighter in her chair.

"That was when I had this gut sense that I was truly doing what I was meant to be doing," she said. "A feeling inside me just confirmed that."

Her work began in a small room with nothing but a computer.

With seed money from her congregation, Sister Joan officially created LifeWay Network, a nonprofit that would provide housing for victims of trafficking and education about the reality of human trafficking, in 2007. LifeWay's first challenge was finding an actual house for the survivors, one that they would be able to keep a secret. At first, Sister Joan tried to leverage one of the many houses owned by different religious communities across the city. Most of them had plenty of rooms to spare, given the aging population of their communities. Nearly all of the orders Sister Joan contacted were willing to offer hospitality to the women on a temporary basis, keeping them safe for a night or two in the very early days after they broke free from their captors. Before long, LifeWay had five convents working with them to provide an Underground Railroad for emergency housing. Soon after, Sister Joan secured a single house that would provide more permanent housing, where women could spend up to a year in order to get on their feet.

"It was kept very quiet," Sister Joan said. "We didn't want people to know what we were doing. The word 'trust' is very important when we speak about victims of human trafficking because it has totally been eradicated and violated for these women. I think the greatest need is the safety; before you have that safety factor, nothing else seems to make sense. They aren't comfortable to try anything else."

Trafficking survivors hide in plain sight. The signs of slavery are vague. "They can include a person who is afraid, doesn't speak the language, has someone else speak for them, a person maybe who has moved several times," Sister Joan explained to me. "Maybe there is no eye contact, signs of bruising. You may think that your maid in your room or your waiter or the woman at the massage parlor all have legit jobs, but in some cases that isn't true. To identify victims of human trafficking is a difficult thing."

Today, LifeWay partners with social-service organizations like Safe Horizons and New York Asian Women's Center to reach out to survivors. When there is a raid or a person is found by law enforcement, officials contact Sister Joan to see if the survivor can live in her safe house.

Staffed by three nuns, a house manager who lives there full-time, and a part-time social worker, the house feels very different from the sterility of a shelter.

"It is a strong sense of community being with the women, rather than it being a boardinghouse kind of thing," Sister Joan explained. "There is somebody at the end of the day who wants to know how you are doing, is everything OK, what was your day like . . . without being intrusive and asking questions about their trafficking situation."

The women come to Sister Joan completely broken, having been abused and tortured physically and mentally. She told me she doesn't push the women to talk to her about what they have gone through. She doesn't need to ask questions to learn about their scars.

"To say a person has been trafficked is to say they have had their freedom taken away from them through force, fraud, or coercion," Sister Joan said. "They are treated like a commodity, not a person, and their humanity is stripped away from them. This is done in insidious ways: abusive behavior, rapes, starvation, the withholding of food, and the forced use of drugs. Sometimes they will be forced to have sex with up to twenty people in a day. That is like a chain around their brain," she says. "The trafficker finds something to hold them. They tell them that their family or their child will be harmed or killed."

The former slaves barely know how to live and behave as free individuals once they are finally out of their captors' grip.

It takes time before they begin to feel safe and move freely as themselves. Safety is the number-one priority at the house, which has one of the best security systems money can buy. The women are instructed to never answer the doors themselves.

The very first woman who walked through the doors of Sister Joan's safe house, a victim of labor trafficking, burst into tears when she saw her very own bed, where she could sleep without worrying that someone would abuse her in the middle of the night.

"Oh my God, this is beautiful," she said, over and over again.

It is beautiful. Sister Joan and her staff were meticulous in making sure that the safe house felt like a home. Every woman has her own bed, her own dresser, her own small night table.

"Setting the house up was one of the fun things we got to do," Sister Joan said with a lilt of delight in her voice. "We had the entire staff hanging curtains, washing windows, and making sure everything was homey and well done." Most of the furniture was donated secondhand, but Sister Joan made sure the beds were brand-new. It was important to her that the women have new beds. LifeWay even created a registry with Target to outfit the home, providing the women with dishes, knives, forks, a toaster, a fridge, even a television. To protect the safe house's location, they had all of the gifts delivered to LifeWay's Forest Hills office. The nuns schlepped everything out to the safe house themselves.

One of the former slaves told Sister Joan that living in the house was like being able to live with her mother all over again. Another young woman was thrown her very first birthday party at the house.

"She had never had a birthday party. You should have seen her face. We had so many candles on the cake, we almost burned the house down. Everyone's face was lit up by all those candles," Sister Joan remembered.

During the day, the women in the safe house work on rebuilding basic life skills, the kind most people take for granted. Many haven't sat at a table to eat in years. In their other lives, they had been forced to sit in corners and beg for food scraps.

"They have been treated like animals," Sister Joan told me, disgusted more by the idea every time we speak about it.

"They were never allowed to come to the table. When they get to us, they are amazed that they are allowed to sit at a table and have real conversations. That is one of the healing parts of the community, the fact that we are all one group, eating together."

Many of them don't speak English at first, so the Life-Way staff teaches them ESL. In the house, English is spoken almost all of the time.

"The main thing in the end is that the women want to be able to work and be independent, and all we do is work to help them achieve that goal," Sister Joan said. "What about education? What is the level of education they need?" They study for their GEDs. One woman recently trained to be a nurse's aide. If they don't have their immigration status, LifeWay works with them and finds a lawyer to assist them. And finally, they try to find a way to prosecute the traffickers who sold them in the first place.

"All of those things are huge; nothing is small," Sister Joan says. "You put the trafficked person in the middle and all the spokes coming out are all the services needed to bring that person back to who they were, to create safety and trust and let them know how precious they are as a human person. All of that is necessary."

Most important, just being around people who don't treat them like property makes them believe they have value again.

There is a lot of darkness in Sister Joan's days. The very idea of human slavery once turned her stomach; now she lives it and breathes it. Instead of wanting to turn away, she told me she wishes she could spend even more time with the women and less time focusing on the administrative tasks that keep the roof over their heads. The key to her stamina is knowing how to unwind.

"I enjoy reading novels," she said. "I love to do my gardening. I exercise every day. For me, the exercise is the key to burning off any negative energy. I notice, when I don't do it, I am crabbier and more tired." The five other Sisters of Halifax with whom she lives help to bolster her spirits. Together they form a family-like unit. "I could never do this kind of work if I didn't have the kind of support that I get from them," Sister Joan says. Each morning they pray together in community. They pray for one another and they pray for the women that Sister Joan protects.

Taking time out for prayer and contemplation is another thing that keeps Sister Joan sane, and the way she enters into a time of prayer makes sense even to someone who isn't at all religious. Prayer, for her, is a time outside the everyday droning of distraction from e-mailing, texting, and decision-making. It is a time of contemplation and silence in a world gone crazy.

She lamented to me that in our modern lives, most people, herself included, have no time to be silent.

"We have iPhones and iPads and i-everything. We are always connected these days. We have no space for quiet unless we carve it out," she said, telling me that she sets aside a special time each day, typically in the morning, for prayer.

Sister Joan changes up how she prays from one day to the next. It can be a meditation on a particular issue or person or it can be less specific, just holding that person or issue in her thoughts. Sister Joan compares a lot of what she does to the Buddhist style of meditation. "It isn't even really thinking about something. It is more holding it and being contemplative. It goes beyond thinking. When we are think-ing, we use our minds. We are trying to control things. We just have to let ourselves contemplate, be still, and let go. It is difficult, but that is God's gift to us. It is like eating and breathing. If I don't set aside time for prayer, I can't live."

Sister Joan became a nun late, relative to the rest of the women I worked with for this book. She never felt the early tug of a calling that most nuns will tell you they experienced in childhood or their early teens.

"I never wanted to be a sister," she says. "When you are a Catholic girl growing up, people always ask you if you want to be a nun. I said no. I always liked a guy too much or liked something else too much." But by joining later in life, she was able to bring rich experiences to a life now devoted completely to God.

One of six kids, with a mom who stayed at home and a dad who worked various jobs as an accountant, never mak-ing much money, Joan lived a simple childhood in England. Looking for a new adventure, Joan moved to Bermuda in her late twenties and soon found work in the island's booming hospitality industry, where she started out as a front-desk clerk and quickly moved up the ranks. She first encoun-tered the poor while working in one of the luxury resorts on the upmarket island. As the general manager's assistant, she ran the personnel department for the hotel, where she met the gardening staff, composed mostly of immigrants from the Azores, as well as the men and women who worked in the kitchens.

"They were so humble and beautiful. I began working with the poorer guys who did the gardens and the people who worked in the kitchens and the back areas, all the parts the [guests] never see, and I got the feeling that these people needed a voice," Sister Joan told me. "I began to feel the draw of religious life mainly because I wanted to work with the poor." She spent less and less time around the island's elite and more and more time with the Sisters of Charity of Halifax, whose focus was on education and caring for the poor. At one point, while living in Bermuda, Joan juggled three different boyfriends, one of whom she knew wanted to marry her.

"I just knew it wasn't enough," she said, in hindsight, of the possibility of getting married. "I know that is an awful thing to say about another human being, but it is true. He just wasn't enough, and I knew that I was meant to do something different."

When she finally joined the Sisters of Charity of Halifax, they gave her the option to choose a community in Nova Scotia, Canada, or in New York City. Sister Joan chose New York because she thought it would be exciting, a new adventure like Bermuda had been, and over the next several years she attended St. John's University before receiving a master's in pastoral studies at Loyola University of Chicago. She ultimately returned to New York City to settle into parish life.

"When people hear about human trafficking, they think it is overseas and faraway. Really, it is very prevalent in the United States," Sister Joan said. But the five boroughs of New York are one of the busiest hubs for trafficking in the United States due to their transient nature, plethora of airports and trains, and a culture where people don't ask too many questions.

Between May and December of 2010, LifeWay Network and Hofstra University's Department of Sociology conducted a survey of service providers and law enforcement agencies to try to determine the number of people trafficked within New York City and to shed light on the need for and availability of social services. Based on data from that survey, they estimated that private service providers in the New York City metropolitan area interacted with at least 11,268 survivors between 2000 and 2010, considerably exceeding previously released official estimates.

Sister Joan worries about money. She operates LifeWay on an annual budget of just $200,000 but is constantly thinking of ways to raise more cash. She has dreams of opening a second safe house and ultimately finding permanent housing and support for survivors. The Hofstra survey found that more survivors would benefit from long-term or transitional housing than they would from emergency housing. But despite this need, they found that safe and affordable long-term housing is virtually nonexistent, with only 3.9 percent of victims who need housing actually receiving it.

In 2012, President Barack Obama made an impassioned commitment to crack down on human trafficking in a campaign speech at the Clinton Global Initiative.

"It is barbaric and it is evil and it has no place in a civilized world," the president told the audience members, among them Queen Rania Al Abdullah of Jordan, Mexican president Felipe Calderón, Rwandan president Paul Kagame, former Secretary of State Condoleezza Rice, and Treasury Secretary Timothy Geithner, at the Sheraton New York Hotel and Towers in Midtown Manhattan. "Nations must speak with one voice: our people and our children are not for sale," he said. That kicked off efforts from the White House to raise awareness of trafficking and to find ways to fund initiatives that could make strides in combatting it. A year later, Sister Joan learned that LifeWay was named a finalist in a competition for $1.8 million in public and private funding that would allow them to open a second safe house for younger women, aged eighteen to twenty-four, and implement new social services to provide them with sustainable aid.

The finalists were told they would participate in a three-day "Innovation Workshop" in Washington, DC, in January 2014, where they would be paired with expert coaches from social enterprise development, technology start-ups, medical and mental health experts, and communications and public relations professionals to further refine their ideas. The winner would be selected later in the year.

"That money would change everything for us," Sister Joan told me breathlessly. "We would be able to focus on more of New York's young people who have been trafficked. We could focus on economic empowerment and bringing them more social services."

One Bible passage in particular stands out for Sister Joan when she tries to put her life's work in perspective. It is a passage from the fourth chapter of the Gospel of Luke, where Jesus declares what God has asked him to do.

The Spirit of the Lord is upon me,
because he has anointed me
to bring good news to the poor.
He has sent me to proclaim release to the captives
and recovery of sight to the blind,
to let the oppressed go free,
to proclaim the year of the Lord's favor.

"That's the one that speaks to the call that I have for the work that I do," she said. "The poor don't always have to be the economically poor. The poor can be those who have suffered tremendous injustice. God's reign is about bringing peace and justice to people. I just work towards providing that."

6.

Keeping an Eye
on Corporate America

*If you own shares in a corporation,
you have a voice, and you need to convince these
corporations to work for the common good.*
—Sister Nora Nash

The last thing anyone expected to go down at the Goldman Sachs 2011 shareholder meeting (typically one of the most staged and staid events on the banking calendar) was for a religious sister to confront CEO Lloyd Blankfein over the excessive amount their executives were being paid that year in the midst of one of the worst recessions to hit the United States in decades.

"Execs have amassed untold wealth while a billion people suffer from poverty and food insecurity," Sister Nora Nash, a small but sturdy woman with an Irish accent, said to the imposing CEO and the room of three hundred Goldman employees and shareholders in a pointedly humble auditorium in Jersey City, New Jersey, across the Hudson River from Goldman's glittering forty-two-story office tower.

Sister Nora was attending the meeting as a shareholder, there to present a resolution to ask the bank's board to evaluate why they paid their top dogs so much money while the rest of the economy floundered. The year prior, the firm's five top executives were paid a total of $69.5 million, impressive in a lackluster year for the company's stock. Yes, 2010 was a good year to be an executive in America. It was a difficult year to be an average American. By the end of the year, median pay for chief executives in the country was rising annually at a rate of 27 percent, while household income was falling by approximately 1 percent.

Addressing Mr. Blankfein, Sister Nora said, "You make more in an hour than most people make in a year." Discussing it later, she told me that she believed Goldman's compensation for its top staff was egregious.

Sister Nora knew her resolution had no chance of passing, but she wanted her voice heard that day. She is a pro at filing shareholder resolutions, and even though the majority of them don't pass, what matters to her is that corporations know she and other socially responsible shareholders are out there—watching them.

"I wanted to speak to the issue of pay disparity between executive compensation and the rest of society," Sister Nora said, explaining why she went after Goldman. "We have millions of people living on the margins of society, and Goldman Sachs is affecting the equity of distribution. Goldman Sachs is at the top of the pyramid, the heart of the financial world, a place where executives have amassed tremendous amounts of wealth, as people at the base of the pyramid are suffering. I asked Goldman Sachs to think about economic justice. I asked them to be a leader."

The bank did in fact reject the shareholder proposal. Their excuse was that the preparation of such a report would be "a distraction" that "would not provide shareholders with any meaningful information." They claimed investors already had all the information they needed about executive pay. A month later, Sister Barbara Aires, the coordinator of corporate responsibility for the Sisters of Charity and a friend and colleague of Sister Nora's, prodded Mr. Blankfein on progress the firm was making on disclosure to their shareholders about their pay packages.

Mr. Blankfein playfully replied that the tone of her questions made her sound like a member of Goldman's management.

Sister Barbara quickly parleyed back, "Do you want to hire me?"

Mr. Blankfein calmly, and with a bit of wit, replied, "I don't think we can outbid your current boss." But what he could do was give them a meeting. And so, months later, Sister Nora and several other shareholder activists were invited across the river to that gleaming tower to meet with Goldman board members about executive compensation. Sister Nora considered that a win.

Nora Nash's job title with the Sisters of St. Francis is Director of Corporate Social Responsibility, which means that she spends her days wading through quarterly reports and earnings statements, participating in dialogues, filing shareholder resolutions, and attending meetings with corporate giants. And as she tells it, this position is her calling from God. She is unwavering in her conviction that corporations have an obligation to act morally. Goldman is just one of dozens of companies that Sister Nora has targeted to up their ante on corporate responsibility. With her at the helm, her congregation has become a force within the world of shareholder activism. She and her assistant director, Tom McCaney, have challenged the grocery store chain Kroger over the rights of farm workers, Hershey's chocolate company over child labor, McDonald's over childhood obesity, Walmart on raising their minimum wage, and Wells Fargo over predatory lending practices. Most recently, they have gotten into the debate over fracking. The list goes on.

Sister Nora hates drawing attention to herself and rarely

grants interviews. I had to e-mail and call about a dozen times before I finally heard back from her.

"I'm horrible at getting to all my e-mails," she explained by way of apology. I took that to mean I should e-mail all the more.

I wrote to her another time, asking for a meeting, and she was hesitant.

"I don't foresee myself as the subject in a book," she wrote. I just kept trying. I became obsessed with meeting this woman who had accomplished what so many of the 99 Percent in the Occupy Wall Street movement that year had been unable to do—get the big banks to answer back. I begged my friend Kevin Roose, a writer for the *New York Times* who had profiled Sister Nora, to give me her phone number.

When I finally got her on the phone, I pushed the subject of how she could possibly shy away from attention after earning so much of it for standing up to Mr. Blankfein at that shareholder meeting. Surely someone who hated the spotlight so much wouldn't have invited that exchange.

"I'm not a person to go in front of cameras. I don't like it. In most cases, I avoid it," she said simply. "In that case, it had to be done."

She finally relented and agreed to meet, telling me I was persistent. She liked that. After we spoke, she warmed to me, at least enough to invite me to come visit her and interview her in person. Just a few days before Christmas, I made the three-hour trip from New York to visit the Our Lady of Angels

Convent, an imposing and beautiful granite structure adjacent to the campus of Neumann University in Aston, Pennsylvania. Sister Nora has perfectly coiffed hair that fades from an almond color to a pale vanilla. She was dressed down that day in a blue cable-knit sweater and seemed delighted to see me, a stark contrast to her terse emails.

"You are fantastic, Jo," she said. I nearly cried from the praise. Nuns know how to give a compliment that warms your soul. She quickly pressed a gift into my hand, a small wooden Tau Cross, Christ's cross in the shape of the Greek letter for *T*, the adopted crest of St. Francis of Assisi; wrapped me in a hug; and insisted on giving me a tour of the grounds and the chapel, simply and elegantly decorated for Christmas.

"You should take a picture with Saint Francis," she urged me as we walked by a life-size bronze statue of her order's namesake, the twelfth-century patron saint of animals, opponent of greed, and fierce and fearless advocate for the poor. "Everyone wants to take a picture with Saint Francis." I did in fact make sure to snap a selfie with the saint before I left for the day.

"This is a wonderful place for contemplation. It was magical when I was a novice here," Sister Nora remarked as we walked through the immaculate hallways and manicured gardens, remembering her early days at the convent more than half a century earlier. The grounds were like a college dormitory back then, she said, with thirty eager young women coming in each year. In 2013, only one new sister joined the congregation. Most of the sisters I met that day were well into their sixth decade. They walked slowly but with intention.

"We have one hundred sisters in a retirement home across the street," Sister Nora said. Many of those women need nursing care. Part of Sister Nora's job is to make sure that the nuns' retirement funds are invested in companies that will not only produce a profit but will work toward the common good of the planet. It isn't exactly how she thought her life would end up.

As a little girl growing up in County Limerick, Ireland, Nora dreamed about becoming a missionary in Africa. She would endlessly thumb through the two missionary magazines in her house, *The Far East* and *Africa,* until they were dog-eared and tattered. She even went door-to-door selling them in elementary school to raise money for the kids on the exotic continent so far away.

"Even as a kid, I was into social justice," she told me. "I didn't know what we were raising money for, except that it would help the tiniest kids in Africa go to school. All I ever really wanted was to act justly, love tenderly, and walk humbly with God." And so her goal was to be a Franciscan missionary in Africa. Her mother put her foot down.

"It was hard to come home from Africa in those days, and my mom just wouldn't accept that," Sister Nora told me with a faraway look in her eye.

One kindly neighbor was a Catholic sister. On days when Nora didn't have to go to school, she would tag along with her to the hospital and volunteer with the patients.

"I liked the work she was doing, and that gave me some of my inspiration," Sister Nora said. There was a Franciscan retreat house not too far away, and when she visited there right after high school, Nora felt the call to become a sister full-time. She soon traveled across the Atlantic Ocean to live in the Franciscan convent outside of Philadelphia.

"I haven't looked back since the Lord called me. We all have our up and down moments, but I have been happy in my life," she told me.

Her first ministry was teaching, and Sister Nora taught every grade all over the Eastern seaboard. She had a ball in Massachusetts, where snowstorms kept the kids home from school for such long stretches that they would actually beg to come in to see their friends and work on the school newspaper. One school in New Jersey was rundown and neglected enough that her provincial superior told her she couldn't possibly make it any worse when she took it over. Two priests had already been assigned to the parish and failed. In just a few years, Sister Nora, with the help of the PTA and two monsignori, made it one of the biggest success stories in the diocese.

Needing a breather, she took a sabbatical and enrolled in postgraduate classes for a year at Notre Dame, which was where she took her first business ethics class, a whisper from the universe that her life was about to turn in an entirely new direction. In the beginning of 2001, her congregation asked her to consider a job she never expected to take on—corporate responsibility ministry. They needed someone to ensure that the order's sizable portfolio and retirement investments were responsibly invested in companies that shared their values. Additionally, she would allocate social justice grants and community development loans.

"It was hard to get someone who was really interested in it," Sister Nora said. "But I was committed to working for justice and working for the common good. I liked the idea of working with corporations, because if we are to share in the benefits of the corporation, then we must actively engage in environmental, social, and governance issues. Corporate responsibility is on our shoulders also."

When a nun takes up the call to put herself into God's service, she doesn't question where that service takes her.

"You just do it. You fulfill the call. God's hand gets involved and then it can move in a different direction," she told me. For the sisters, corporate responsibility involved monitoring their investment portfolio from a moral and ethical perspective and then exercising their rights and responsibilities as shareholders to hold corporations accountable for their policies and practices. "For us, that means a deep consciousness of human rights, environmental rights, and the increasing consciousness of sustainability," she said.

When they took a close look at their investment portfolio, some sisters were troubled by what they saw as irresponsible investing. Religious communities had amassed sizable pension funds by the 1980s, and they were making some smart investments. They really had no choice. Even then, it was clear that their populations were aging faster than they were adding to their ranks and they would need funds to care for the sisters as they grew older.

The Sisters of St. Francis of Philadelphia partnered with ICCR, the Interfaith Center on Corporate Responsibility— an umbrella group of religious organizations that pool their funds to have more clout with the companies they target for responsible management.

"We're not some fly-by-night group filing a resolution," Sister Nora said. "ICCR is a highly respected organization whose members manage major pension funds and billion-dollar asset management organizations. I do think that the fact that we come at the cases from a place of faith shows that we are presenting the truth and aiming for good in society." She knows when to use faith to her advantage. She is quick with a good Bible joke, for example. Some of her favorites include:

Q: Who was the greatest female financier?
A: Pharaoh's daughter. She went to the bank of the Nile
   and drew out a tiny prophet.

Q: Who was the greatest babysitter in the Bible?
A: David. He rocked Goliath to sleep.

Q: Why didn't they play cards on the Ark?

A: Because Noah was standing on the deck.

As a matter of taste and morals, the Sisters of St. Francis of Philadelphia don't invest in companies that deal in things like tobacco, gambling, or pornography unless they are trying to motivate a company to change. They also typically avoid sizable investments in defense contractors. But when the congregation wants to try to change a company, they invest just a modicum of money—the minimum amount the SEC requires for them to be considered shareholders is $2,000. And so they own $2,000 worth of stock in companies like Philip Morris, R. J. Reynolds, Lockheed Martin, and Boeing. They have worked with Philip Morris on drawing up agricultural policies to protect tobacco farmers in Malawi from pesticides, with Lockheed Martin on human rights issues, with Chevron on fracking, and with Walgreens to try to convince them to stop selling cigarettes.

"They sat right here in this conference room and told us that they would love to stop selling cigarettes, but it is just too high a percentage of their business," Sister Nora told me with a shake of her head and a wave of her arm around the convent's finely appointed conference room and imposing mahogany table. Surrounding the table are framed photographs of the order's leaders staring down at the room's occupants in what could alternately be described as judgment or curiosity. Mother Mary Francis has the wall to the right of the room's doorway all to herself. The founder of the Sisters of St. Francis of Philadelphia was born Maria Anna Boll Bachmann in Bavaria. She had three children and was pregnant with a fourth when she was widowed in 1851. Together with her sister Barbara and a novice in the Franciscan Secular Third Order, Maria Anna asked Bishop John Neumann to establish a congregation of Franciscan sisters in their diocese, and she became Sister Mary Francis, the first Mother Superior of the order. During the second half of the nineteenth century, the sisters served God wherever they saw a need. They supported themselves by taking in piecemeal sewing jobs, making just enough money to live and nurse the sick and the poor in their congregation.

Moving clockwise around that very conference room today, the next wall bears the superiors who succeeded Mother Mary Francis at the latter end of the nineteenth century, stoic women in full habits, only two-thirds of their faces peeking through the heavy black cloth. Then it is as though an imaginary line were drawn in between the photographs taken from the 1960s to 1970s. As I stared at it with confusion, Sister Nora looked at me. "Vatican II," she said. No longer did the sisters in the photographs wear the dark habits. They switched first to a modified habit and veil and then surrendered them altogether, donning smart suits with brightly colored blouses.

The majority of the Franciscan sisters' funds are invested in Fortune 500 companies that behave responsibly—they are transparent, upstanding members of their communities, fair in their compensation practices and mindful of human rights. But even those corporations could often do better. Sister Nora isn't afraid to stand her ground when she thinks that a company is not up to snuff.

Back in 2011, ICCR members, including Sister Nora, almost walked right out of a meeting with Hershey at their corporate headquarters in central Pennsylvania. "They were just stalling rather than dialoguing with us, and we were about to say, 'Let's get out of here.' All we wanted was for them to produce one product without child labor. We were begging them to produce one product without child labor," she told me.

Since that meeting, Sister Nora says, the chocolate company has come a long way. With her nudging, along with that of the ICCR and other activist shareholders, Hershey's pledged to source their cocoa from responsible co-op farms. In Christmas of 2012 the company released their first chocolate bar made entirely without child labor, and they have pledged to be completely free of child labor by 2020. Right before I visited her, Sister Nora was able to get on a group call with a farmer in Ghana, who told her that working conditions had vastly improved.

"We are just thrilled," she told me. "Some people will say, 'Oh, 2020 is a long way off.' I say you have to have goals!"

The goal is always to get a face-to-face meeting with executives. That's how you get the best answers. ICCR members collaborate on goals for different issues and always find that the best path is through dialogue with upper management and executives, when it's possible. They research company policies, write letters, meet face-to-face, do conference calls, and file resolutions when necessary. When it comes to her work, Sister Nora is a relentless communicator, which is why most corporations have found that it is simply easier to schedule a meeting with her rather than open themselves up to the very public criticism that comes when the nun files a resolution against the company that legally must be read at a shareholder meeting. Sister Nora isn't sure whether the executives respond to her differently because she is a nun or because she represents a group that controls some very sizable investments and the ICCR is very well respected.

"Corporations have learned to respect us, not just because we sit on the other side of the table, but because we represent the interests of the investor, the communities, and the corporation. If you don't do what is right and just, you're damaging your reputation and your shareholders'," she explained. "They know we're speaking from a place of truth."

Sister Nora speaks often about bringing the Franciscan spirit into her work, a message that is categorically straightforward: greed produces suffering. Her order's namesake,

Giovanni di Pietro di Bernardone, nicknamed Francesco, or Francis, was raised in an upper-middle-class family with a luxury clothmaker for a father. After witnessing the poor beggars on the streets of Rome, Francis made the choice to forego the trappings of the upper class in order to live and work among the sick and the poor as a preacher. "Remember that when you leave this Earth, you can take with you nothing that you have received—only what you have given," Francis wrote.

In addition to the teachings of Saint Francis, Sister Nora looks to the Bible to provide a value base for promoting the common good, human dignity, human rights, sustainability, and overall corporate responsibility. As a Sister of St. Francis of Philadelphia, she is deeply committed to what her congregation calls "the care for creation," which includes protecting and defending the rights of those who are poor and vulnerable, and who stand to be most severely affected by environmental degradation and climate change.

"Matthew 5 is a biggie," she told me. That verse is the start of the well-known Sermon on the Mount, where Jesus gathers his disciples around him to teach them the value of social justice:

> *Blessed are the poor in spirit, for theirs is the kingdom of heaven.*
> *Blessed are those who mourn, for they shall be comforted.*
> *Blessed are the gentle, for they shall inherit the earth.*

Blessed are those who hunger and thirst for righteousness,
for they shall be satisfied.
Blessed are the merciful, for they shall receive mercy.
Blessed are the pure in heart, for they shall see God.
Blessed are the peacemakers, for they shall be called sons
of God.
Blessed are those who have been persecuted because of righ-
teousness, for theirs is the kingdom of heaven.

Corporations, Sister Nora tells me, have so much control over the lives of ordinary people, the meek, the hungry, and the poor, that they should have a responsibility to take care of them.

Sister Nora prays daily. Her local convent gathers for Morning Prayer at 6:30 a.m., but she rises even earlier for her own personal prayer at home. The sisters try to pray together each night, but that can get difficult with everyone's hectic schedules. She attends church every day except Monday, when there is no liturgy in her local parish. Instead she goes to physical therapy.

Our time together at the convent came to an end just before dusk. Sister Nora needed to leave me in order to check her phone messages. She had been playing a bothersome game of phone tag with Wells Fargo Bank on the day that I met her at the convent. When it comes to shareholder activism, you have to cross every *t* and dot every *i*. Corporations will look for any loophole to try to ignore your resolution. Sister Nora wasn't having it. She stressed that the sisters were very qualified to ask their questions, as they were continuous holders of the bank's stock.

"You're pretty fierce," I told her.

She smiled almost shyly back at me.

"You have to be," she said, and winked. "I have a passion for justice."

7.

The Act of Survival Is Worse Than the Torture Itself

Torture does not end with the release from some clandestine prison.
—Sister Dianna Mae Ortiz

Sister Dianna Mae Ortiz had only been working as a missionary in San Miguel, Guatemala, for a few months when the death threats began. She had no clue what provoked them. Sister Dianna was just a nun in her twenties, there to teach elementary school English and hardly a threat to anyone.

"You are going to die in this country. Return to your country," one menacing letter read.

A second notice was composed of words cut from a newsletter and glued to a piece of stationery, looking almost farcical, like something out of a movie, except for the chilling command:

> *Eliminate Dianna. Raped, disappeared, decapitates leave the country.*

She was terrified but didn't want to make the threats public for fear of word reaching her parents back in New Mexico, whom she knew would demand that she come home and give up on this adventure.

"It isn't easy for me to admit, but fear clawed its way into my life and began to affect my physical health and my ministry. I began fearing the people who were part of my community," Sister Dianna told me some twenty years later.

She had a reason to be afraid. She should have been more afraid.

It isn't easy to tell Sister Dianna's story. In so many ways she is a woman still painfully broken from her experience in Guatemala all those years ago. Just speaking about it brings her intense psychological pain, while her every movement reminds her of the physical pain inflicted on her young body. She is a survivor who has channeled a terrible experience into a way to help others. For that and for many other reasons I am in awe of her. What follows was difficult for her to tell me, hard for me to hear from Sister Dianna's mouth, challenging to write, and may be problematic for the sensitive reader.

When she first traveled to the Central American country in 1987, Sister Dianna Mae Ortiz, a young Ursuline nun from New Mexico with clear, bright, coffee-colored eyes; a toothy smile embedded into delicate features; and dark curly hair, planned to live in Guatemala for the rest of her life.

"I thought I would breathe my last breath there," she told me the first time we spoke in 2012. Fiercely dedicated to the children there, she loved the people like family and taught them Spanish in the hopes that they could one day pull themselves out of the worst kind of poverty. She never wanted to do anything else except live among these people and serve God. When Dianna was just six years old, her parents asked each of her siblings what they wanted to be when they grew up. Dianna didn't blink or pause like the other kids. "A nun," she said with a casino dealer's certainty. She just kept saying it too, to anyone who would listen, which forced her into a kind of social isolation. The girls in her school teased her. In junior high and high school they crossed themselves and laughed when she walked by, but she ignored them, feeling strong and confident in what she wanted to do with her future.

During her junior year, as other kids were filling out college applications, Dianna began to put her plan into action. She visited an Ursuline sister who was the principal of a local school to inquire about how she could become a nun. That sister invited her to the Ursuline motherhouse in Maple Mount, Kentucky. She spent her senior year at the girls' school there and went on to a nearby Catholic college to receive a degree in education, making her temporary vows with the Ursulines before she graduated. Sister Dianna finally felt at home.

Once she settled into convent life, the teasing continued, but in a good-natured way that no longer bothered her. Her nicknames in the convent were "The Prima Donna" and "Lady Di." She was modest and neat, with clothes always perfectly ironed. There she developed strong friendships that would last her entire life. Once she became a sister, all Sister Dianna wanted to do was serve as a missionary in Central America. With parents of Spanish and Mexican heritage, she felt called to learn more about her family's history and travel to a place where she could immerse herself in Hispanic culture.

In 1987 her wish was granted when she was sent to work as a missionary in a small indigenous village in Guatemala. It took forty-four hours by bus from Mexico City to reach Guatemala City. From there she left for San Miguel Acatán, a cripplingly poor rural Mayan village, where 80 percent of the population under the age of five suffered from malnutrition, to teach grade-school children how to read and write. She learned a few phrases in the local dialect, K'anjobal, and set out to convince the wary villagers that she was there to stay. They were distrustful. For five hundred years these people had watched as foreigners came to their country, took what they wanted, and walked away. "Everyone who has come here has left us," they told her. "You're not going to abandon us too?"

"No, I will never leave you," she told them.

Sister Dianna expected to teach kindergarten, ages five to seven, but there were so few teachers that she ended up with a class of students from ages three to fourteen. Many of them had never held a pencil, seen a book, or used a crayon before. Because her initial intention was to teach them in Spanish, she had gone to language training for several months to become fluent. It was quickly apparent that speaking to the Mayan children in Spanish was useless.

"What I later learned was that education is a threat to governments," Sister Dianna told me. "When someone teaches people to read and write and be proud of who they are, it teaches them to demand more from a society than brutal oppression. They become dangerous." So she worked with the local women to create a system of translation— from the kids to a translator to her—and then reversed it.

Guatemala in the 1980s was a dangerous place. In 1982, the violent overthrow of the government led the military to take their aggression out on poor indigenous people in the countryside, the very people Sister Dianna was ministering to. The Army unleashed a scorched-earth campaign designed to destroy anyone viewed as an insurgent against the government and obliterated 440 rural villages. Human rights organizations estimated that as many as 100,000 Guatemalans were abducted or killed by their own government in the 1980s. Torture, disappearances, and massacres were routine. Anyone considered a threat was eliminated. Many of the victims were women. Most of the people who disappeared were found dead. Priests and religious workers were regularly hunted down and killed by an army that viewed them as allies of the guerillas, as well as Communist sympathizers.

When Sister Dianna first arrived, the people in San Miguel told her a story: The military had come in one day and told the women they would be killed if they didn't cook them tortillas. When they had cooked the tortillas, the guerillas came to the village to cut their heads off for cooking for the military. The village, they said, had no allies on either side.

Despite all that, many of Sister Dianna's memories of her early days in the village were happy ones. She remembers fondly her walks with the children and how they collected stones to build miniature prayer altars for her. On the days they did not walk, the children would knock on the nun's door and then bolt away quickly when she answered, leaving their small offering of stones outside the doorframe.

"It was symbolic," she recalled. "[The children] were my rocks."

By the time the threats arrived, she was committed to these people, but Sister Dianna knew that as a foreigner she had an easy way out. Americans could always just go home, where the threats would never follow them, and it would be written off as a journey gone wrong. She would have other adventures. But what gnawed at her was whether she could leave all those children with whomever was placing her life in danger.

Ultimately, Sister Dianna didn't think it was her decision to make—it was God's. She made retreats and prayed for hours on end. One day, reading the Bible in the garden of the retreat house with her friend Sister Darleen, she dared the book to fall open to any passage. When it landed, spine flat on the ground and pages open to the sky, staring at her was the story of Jeremiah, the prophet who remained with his people despite his persecution by his friends and family. The officials and the nobles of Babylon "took Jeremiah out of the court of the guardhouse and entrusted him to Gedaliah, the son of Ahikam, the son of Shaphan, to take him home. So he stayed among the people."

She had her answer. God was telling her not to flee.

"I remember my eyes resting on that page and there was a moment of indescribable peace, like an embrace from God. I knew that the road I would be walking down, I would not be walking alone. There was my answer. I knew I would stay with the people of Guatemala," she told me.

On the morning of November 2, 1989, Sister Dianna was on another religious retreat in the neighboring village of Antigua. A scruffy man wearing a *Rambo* T-shirt appeared in the garden behind the retreat house with a gun in one pocket and a hand grenade in the other. He swiftly reached out and grabbed the young nun, yanking her violently through a hole in the wall. "Please, God, let this be a dream," she remembers thinking as he blindfolded her. "*Hola mi amor!* We have some things to discuss," the man said.

Her captor threatened to release a hand grenade if she did not board a public bus with him. So she did. The bus stopped in the small town of Mixco, where the man and two compatriots escorted her to a waiting car. There were three captors—a man named Jose and two others, whom she nicknamed "The Policeman" and "The Guate-man" to keep them straight in her head. "Guate-man" is short for a man from Guatemala City. Sister Dianna was terrified to realize that she recognized him from a recent trip she had made to the city to run errands. He had walked up next to her on a busy street and grabbed her by the arm. "We know who you are. We know where you live," he had hissed in her ear. Jose was a dark-skinned Mayan man with matted hair and a bad eye. He was the first to introduce himself once they arrived at a compound that she would later describe as a secret prison.

"They tell me you are a nun. Is that true?" Jose asked her once he had her locked in a cell in a dilapidated building in the middle of nowhere. "I go to church every Sunday and read the Holy Bible every day. Since you are a nun, surely you must know if God forgives people for the sins they have committed. I don't like my work. But I have a wife. I have children. . . . Sometimes we live at the expense of others."

Jose believed that the presence of a sister elevated the dingy jail cell into a confessional booth. A spigot was opened and stories of his sins poured out of him like raw sewage from a gutter. He described raiding a town in the north of the country. There he armed each of the boys in that village with a can of gasoline and told them to douse their own homes and light them on fire. Petrified, a small boy clasped his mother's skirt, paralyzed. An older man begged Jose to be allowed to take the little boy's place. So, Jose told Sister Dianna, he slammed the two of them in the head with the butt of his rifle. The small boy's head split in two halves like a ripe watermelon. The rest of the children did as they were told and turned their town to ash.

"We took the women to the chapel. I hate to tell you what we did to them," he told the nun, his breath hot against her skin. "Old women, young girls, very young, pregnant women."

He seemed proud before catching a flash of remorse. "I did not want to do it. I have nothing against you, *Madre*. Can you forgive me?" he asked. "If you, a nun, can forgive me, maybe God, too, can forgive me."

Sister Dianna didn't know where she was. She didn't know if this man would let her live or be the one to kill her. What was the right answer? Was there even a right answer? She told him he would have to ask for forgiveness from God and from those whose lives he had silenced. He didn't like that. "I am sorry, *Madre*. I could have saved you," he said. "If you had forgiven me, I could have saved you."

First came her interrogation. They played a "game." If

she answered a question the way they liked, she would be allowed to smoke a cigarette. If they didn't like what she said, they would burn her with it.

Next, Sister Dianna was suspended over a pit full of bodies—men, women, children, some decapitated, all caked in blood. Some were still alive. Moaning. Rats ran across the bodies and swarmed Sister Dianna as she was suspended over the top of the pit, held aloft by her bruised wrists.

There was just one source of strength for her in that hellhole: her cellmate, a woman who had been severely tortured. From a cot across the room, the woman turned her head and tried to smile at Sister Dianna. Her breasts had been cut open. Maggots swarmed inside them. Sensing that the woman needed to feel her touch, Sister Dianna moved toward her and grabbed her hand.

But perhaps Sister Dianna needed the woman more than the woman needed her. "Dianna, be strong. They will try to break you," the woman whispered through cracked and bloodied lips. The nun would repeat those words over and over again in her head. Three words—Dianna, Be Strong—kept her from completely abandoning faith that people could be good. "In that prison cell, where I witnessed the near-death of my faith, I made a promise to her and to the others who were there that I would tell the world what I had witnessed," Sister Dianna told me.

She lay with the woman for several hours before all three of her captors burst into the cell. She describes what happened next as her soul's darkest moment, the moment she felt crushed by Satan. "Everything that made my life worth living withered. Hope vanished. I became a lost spirit in a world that didn't make sense," she said.

One of the men walked toward Sister Dianna and handed her a machete, then stood behind her and trapped her hands beneath his. He placed his callused hands over hers and forced her to stab at the woman over and over again. She couldn't stop him. His full weight bore down on her tiny hands. She could only look away and sob.

Then they gambled for Sister Dianna's body.

"Heads I go first, tails you go," one said. "Heads. She's mine."

Sister Dianna shifted her weight into him, softened her rigid stance, and commanded her hands to touch his body.

"Hey, she wants me," the captor bragged.

She'd had enough. She mustered all of the grit she wished she'd had when they forced her to harm the woman. She stepped quickly backward, thrusting her knee with all of the strength of her five-foot frame into his groin. He tossed her to the floor like a bale of hay.

"Forgive me, please. Give me another chance," she begged. A fist rammed into her stomach.

He climbed on top of her and tore at her clothes, reeking of alcohol, cigarettes, and body odor.

"I want to see your pretty face," he said, snatching her blindfold away while he slid his slimy tongue across her eyelids, nose, and cheeks. He pried open her eyes and ripped her jeans and underwear off. His eyes were just black holes, devoid of any emotion.

As he finished, he whispered in her ear, "*Gracias*. Your God is dead."

They blindfolded her and prepared to rape her again, yelling out in Spanish to a new man. This one was tall with fair skin. He responded in perfect English and with no trace of an accent, "Shit!"

In broken Spanish, he began swearing. "Idiots! She's a North American nun and it is all over the news."

"Are you American?" Sister Dianna asked the new man.

"Why do you want to know?" he answered her in Spanish.

He had her clothes brought to her and helped her put on her T-shirt and sweatshirt.

"Come on. Let's get out of here," he said, as if it had been an option she could have exercised all along, as if the door to freedom had always been just a polite question and a few steps away.

"I'm sorry, so sorry. It was a mistake," he said, leading her down a long hallway. "You must forgive them. They had the wrong person. They thought you were Veronica Ortiz Hernandez."

She knew they didn't think she was Veronica Ortiz Hernandez. Ms. Hernandez was a leftist guerilla freedom fighter. The death threats she received were addressed to Madre Dianna, not Veronica Ortiz.

The man Sister Dianna suspected of being an American ushered her into the passenger seat of a gray Suzuki jeep with a rabbit's foot dangling from the rearview mirror. His hair was brown, curly, and too shiny. She suspected it was a wig.

"I'll take you to a friend at the US embassy who can help you leave the country," he said over classical music playing on the radio. "We tried to warn you with threats to prevent this. You wouldn't leave." Anger tinged his voice.

"I stayed because I have a commitment to the people," she said.

"I have a commitment to the people too, to liberate them from Communists."

"Your commitment is different because you don't respect human life," she replied.

Why was she arguing with him? She couldn't stop herself. She began to wonder whether they were actually heading for the US embassy. Why would he tell her these things and then set her free?

Sister Dianna looked around. The traffic was picking up. She saw a sign for Zone 5. Zone 5 meant they were close to the capital.

At a red light, the American slowed the car. She opened the door and jumped out, bracing herself as she hit the pavement. She ran as fast as she could. She didn't look back.

She ran straight into an indigenous woman. "Sister Dianna," the woman said, apparently recognizing her from the news.

"I escaped," Sister Dianna was able to cough.

"Come with me," the woman said, and grabbed her arm. "You'll be safe."

The woman guided her into a little house and brought her chamomile tea and a plate of beans and tortillas. Her body was numb and tears gushed down her cheeks. The woman told Sister Dianna to rest and pray, but she felt she needed a plan. She needed to leave the country. Her passport was all the way in Zone 1, locked in the manager's desk at Hayter's Travel. Sister Dianna told her host she needed to get to Zone 1. The woman gave her directions and bus fare. "Don't tell anyone anything about me," she warned as she said good-bye.

Once at the travel agency, Sister Dianna was able to call Sister Darleen and was moved to the Vatican embassy. The next three days, she bathed every hour, spending the rest of the time facedown in bed.

The headlines all said "US Nun Released." She wanted to tell them that that wasn't true. She wasn't released. She escaped. She didn't know whom to tell. She didn't know who would believe her.

Her torturers had told her repeatedly that no one would ever believe her story, and as it turns out, they were right. The Guatemalan government was quick to deny any involvement in her kidnapping. "What happened to Dianna Ortiz was self-kidnapping," the stories in Guatemala said.

According to General Carlos Morales, the minister of the interior for Guatemala: "In no moment did police authorities have anything to do with this incident and for this reason the government has closed the case." Guatemalan defense minister Hector Gramajo told an Americas Watch investigator that Sister Dianna was abducted when she snuck out to meet a lesbian lover. Gramajo called her accusations a big injustice to Guatemala and to its security forces.

The Bush administration, too, doubted Sister Dianna's credibility.

In one cable to Washington, then-ambassador Thomas F. Stroock, a newly arrived political appointee of the president, wrote that he rejected her claim that the man who led her out of the secret prison was a North American who spoke Spanish poorly and cursed in English.

"I know something happened to her in Guatemala," Mr. Stroock told *Washington Post* reporter Frank Smyth over the phone from Wyoming. "What I don't know is what it was. I don't know whether to believe her or not."

"I felt betrayed," Sister Dianna later told me through anguished tears. "I don't think I have ever really shared with people how betrayed and hurt I felt by my country and my government. I think I learned to hide my feelings. I had more than a hundred and eleven cigarette burns on my back and elsewhere. I had proof," she said. "When I think of their accusations, those words are like having cigarettes put out on my body all over again."

She was taken to her parents' home in Grants, New Mexico, her mind foggy and thick with amnesia from PTSD caused by the trauma. Sister Dianna described all of her memories as intermingled with the torture.

"Every part of me ceased to exist," she said.

When she walked through the small adobe house, a woman she didn't recognize fell at her feet.

"*Mi Hijita*," she wailed. It was her mother. Sister Dianna backed away. A man, her father, threw his arm around her. He reeked of cigarettes, which only served to remind her of the burns freckling her back and shoulder blades. In that moment, the smell of burning flesh overwhelmed her. She kept her mouth shut, pretended to know them.

When she returned to her community of sisters, she couldn't remember having been a nun.

"For a while I thought I didn't belong in this community because I didn't have memories, and I thought, Why am I here if I don't remember?" she said. But the sisters were supportive. They shared pictures and letters she had written to them. She slowly began to remember that she became a sister because she wanted to be of service.

In the years after her torture, Sister Dianna looked to the words of Jean Améry, an Austrian essayist and philosopher who was tortured by the Nazis. "Gone was the God to whom I had committed my life. Gone was trust, the very idea of justice betrayed. Gone was all I had believed in. Everything that defined me as a human being ceased to exist," he wrote about his own experience. Améry's words brought her comfort. She, too, still felt tortured and uneasy about living in the world. The words seemed written just for her. She took comfort in there being another person on Earth who understood what she went through at the hands of her torturers. Years later she learned that Jean Améry had killed himself. Many times she thought about how easy it would be to take that option herself and end all of her pain.

She had two years of therapy at the Marjorie Kovler Center for the Treatment of Survivors of Torture, the first community-based comprehensive torture treatment center for refugees and people seeking asylum in the United States. It was there that she figured out how to put her experience in perspective and began to find her voice.

In 1996, Sister Dianna camped outside the White House for several weeks, surviving only on bread and water. She wanted the government to acknowledge what had happened to her and to the Guatemalan people.

"Prior to that time I had been trying to obtain information about my case and I was calling on President Clinton and the US government to release documents related to torture in Guatemala," she explained. She began her silent vigil in Lafayette Park across from the White House, joined sporadically by hundreds of supporters. President Clinton wrote to her on March 29, promising to release "all appropriate information" to her. Sister Dianna spent most of her time sitting silently on a blanket.

On April 5, then First Lady and future Secretary of State Hillary Clinton met with Sister Dianna for a half hour to express her concern and assure her that her husband was determined to get her the information she was seeking.

Sister Dianna only broke down once in front of Mrs. Clinton, while she was discussing how her torturers forced her to put her hands on a machete and cut her fellow captive. A few classified documents were eventually released, accompanied by considerable publicity, but they remained heavily redacted and the identity of her torturers was not revealed.

For her own sanity, Sister Dianna Mae Ortiz had to find a way to move on, a way to put her own ordeal behind her.

"For a lot of years I directed my energy to Guatemala and I thought only of the Guatemalan people. Because of the horror I witnessed, I think I was blind to the torture happening all over the rest of the world," she said. But then she began to meet other survivors, ordinary people: aid workers, engineers, accountants, doctors, student activists from all over the United States, Asia, the Middle East, and South America.

"Through them, a sort of blindfold was lifted from my eyes. I saw that torture was a worldwide epidemic and I realized the importance of founding an organization that was comprised entirely of survivors of torture who could help one another."

That realization led Sister Dianna to create the Torture Abolition and Survivors Support Coalition, or TASSC, in 1998. It was a group that allowed torture survivors to speak openly about their experiences as a way to heal. They spoke out to spread the word about torture around the globe and provided torture survivors and their families with legal, psychological, and medical support.

The goal was lofty: to ensure that what happened to them would not happen to anyone ever again. On June 26, 2000, Sister Dianna traveled with eighteen other survivors of torture, from all over the world, to speak with an official of the National Security Council. In a pale-green room in the Old Executive Office Building, just west of the White House, all eighteen of them pled for an end to the US funding and practicing of torture around the globe.

"People tend to think that when a person manages to escape from a situation of torture, it is just like the end to any other story. But . . . for the majority of survivors, the act of survival is far worse than the torture itself," Sister Dianna told me.

In 2002, Sister Dianna wrote a memoir entitled *The Blindfold's Eyes*. More than 500 pages long, it features a picture of her on the cover, a small cross at her collarbone, her eyes laden with an inescapable pain. In 2010, she wrote to President Barack Obama to ask for the president's leadership in ending the country's involvement in any kind of torture anywhere in the world.

That letter went viral when the actress Mariska Hargitay, a star of the series *Law and Order: SVU*, read it aloud at a fund-raiser.

"Dear President Obama, on November 2, 1989, I was

burned with cigarettes more than 111 times," Sister Dianna had written. "I was raped over and over again, and that was only the beginning. Mr. President, from anonymous graves voices still cry out. . . . Torture does not end with the release from some clandestine prison. It is not something we 'get over.' Simply looking forward is not an option for us . . . memories cling to us. . . . No one fully recovers from torture. The damage can never be undone. We have been beaten, hanged by wrists, arms, or legs, burned by electrical devices or cigarettes, bitten by humans and dogs, cut or stabbed with knives or machetes. And this is only a sample of what has been done to us. What a cruel irony that it is the tortured one and not the torturer who feels shame."

For more than ten years, Sister Dianna served as the director of TASSC. In 2012, she decided she needed to take some time for herself to continue her own healing process. Nevertheless, the idea of taking any kind of time for herself makes her uneasy.

"I kind of feel guilty about it," she told me. "The idea of just being able to be still and breathe is frightening."

I had sent Sister Dianna an e-mail with my questions before we spoke because she told me she had difficulty remembering some of the things that had happened to her and thinking about the questions ahead of time helps to jog her memory. One of the questions I wanted to ask her was whether she had any regrets. Once we got on the phone, she told me she thought about that question for a long time before she was ready for our interview.

"Even after all these years, I still travel back in time and I continue to ask the same questions. What would Jesus have done under those circumstances? And each time, the answer remains the same: He would have continued to journey with the people. I have no regrets about the situation," she said, her voice cracking. "Am I happy my dignity and human rights were violated? Am I happy that the brutal acts of those who are children of God shattered my life to the point that I am afraid of my own shadow? Of course not.

"I am not comparing myself to Jesus. I try to follow the Gospel and live the Gospel. But I do believe that on some level I took my place on what I refer to as a modern-day cross. I see the world with new eyes."

8.

I Want to Run a Laundromat Before I Die

*If we really believe in the resurrection, then we have
to believe in second chances. Nobody comes out of prison saying,
"Wow, I really hope I screw up again."*

—Sister Tesa Fitzgerald

I love going to prison," Sister Tesa Fitzgerald told me as we strolled down Twelfth Street and onto Thirty-Seventh Avenue in Long Island City, Queens. "You can taste the hope in the prisons. The women are appreciative and welcoming. You get a real sense that people are working to change their lives."

Everyone for a ten-block radius knew Sister Tesa. They belted out, "Hey Sister T!" and in turn she would greet them by name with bear hugs. Even the neighborhood stray cats curled themselves around her legs as she walked with a measured gait. She knew their names too. Sister Tesa is the honorary mayor of this neighborhood just a half mile inland from the East River, tucked behind the red-and-white striped smokestacks of the Con Edison power plant.

This is Hour Children territory, Sister Tesa's nonprofit dedicated to helping moms connect with their kids while they serve time in prison and then aiding them in the rebuilding of their lives and families when they are back on the outside. The name "Hour Children" comes from the fact that jailed mothers get only an hour at a time to visit with their kids.

We stopped to greet one of Sister Tesa's employees on the street. Almost everyone who works for her, in her hair salon, her food bank, and her thrift shops, is a former felon. Sister Tesa shuttles back and forth between her home and office in Long Island City to prisons in upstate New York on a weekly basis. The outpouring of love for Sister T is the same at the prisons, where the guards all know her name. The inmates cheer when she walks down the corridor, pressing notes of gratitude into her hands.

She cries with the women who don't know whether their kids will want to see them or speak to them again. When babies are born in the prison, Sister Tesa is the one who takes them out of its walls for the first time and she raises them as her own until the women are released.

Sister Tesa works with an annual budget of $3.6 million—a mixture of grants, donations, and government funding she refers to with a growly laugh as "grant stew"—and she is adamant that it is never enough. With that money the Hour Children staff and an army of volunteers run five communal homes, where former felons can live with their children once they are released. From prison halls to the outside, they are a full-service operation. Over the past twenty-five years, Hour Children has provided help to more than nine thousand mothers and raised thousands of children. Sister Tesa starts as an advocate in the prison, providing counseling to get the women ready for the real world. Once they are released, she takes care of everything and anything that could be a stumbling block for these women, from finding affordable housing to securing a job, finding the right doctors, and obtaining the right medication. No detail of a woman's life is overlooked. They are given clothes, taken to the salon, and taught computer skills and even office manners.

The difference Hour Children makes is clear. More than 29 percent of New York State's female ex-convicts are eventually rearrested. For women taken in by Hour Children, that number drops to 3 percent.

Sister Tesa's office is always cluttered, but during the holiday season it is packed with toys, bikes with training wheels, Barbie dolls, video games, and the odd Rainbow Loom—all for the kids in the program. The walls are a panorama of photographs of children, ranging from wallet-size to eight-by-tens. There are girls in dance costumes, boys smiling with gaps in their teeth, high school graduates, and babies—so many babies.

"They're all my babies," Sister Tesa told me in her thick Long Island accent that waxes and wanes depending on whom she is talking to. Put her in front of a local politician and she drops almost all of her r's and g's. This mix of babies—black, white, Latino—belongs to the prisoners who have gone through her programs. The photos trip over one another, and as I gazed at the wall, she named each child and told their story. Julia, just eight years old in her photo, has since gone to college at the University of Vermont and lives in New Jersey where she is now "engaged to a wonderful man." Cyrus is a handful, but he just got the best report card in his class. All over the room are Catholic tchotchkes, including a candy jar in the shape of a nun that reads HEAVENLY HABIT, and a small sculpture of two nuns in full conservative dress wearing sunglasses and riding a motorcycle. The inscription reads, IF YOU FOLLOW ALL THE RULES, YOU MISS ALL THE FUN.

"Isn't that the truth?" Sister Tesa said with a laugh when she noticed I was reading it. "We break the rules all the time." Two cats purred at her feet. Richie, the gray one, and Romy, the black one. They could have fit into a teacup when one of Sister Tesa's volunteers gave them to her eight years ago. Now they live the life, each with his own wicker bed at opposite ends of the nun's office. They drink out of a fishbowl that has no fish. "They're my partners," Sister Tesa told me, reaching down and stroking Richie's back. They're always here and they're part of the action. Everyone associates me with them and them with me."

The furniture in the office is all secondhand. "I barely ever buy anything," she announced proudly, running her hand over her desk. The Hour Children empire includes three thrift shops in Queens, all staffed by former felons and filled wall-to-wall and floor-to-ceiling with inventory. Everything from a white baby grand piano to a sheared beaver cape to an armoire believed to be from Brittany in France is there looking for a new home.

The largest of the stores used to be a nightclub called Studio 34, which some of the neighbors described as "hell on earth." Sister Tesa noticed a For Rent sign at the closed club while she was on one of her walks around the neighborhood, on a hunt for a bagful of her favorite samosas. She made a good deal with the landlord of the defunct club and turned it into a new revenue stream.

"We needed to get rid of four bars, a dance floor, and a lot of questionable rooms in the basement," Sister Tesa told me about gutting the old hotspot. "I don't want to know what they did down there in that basement." She gave me a very knowing look to indicate she knew exactly what was going on in that basement. When it was finished, every square inch was used to move secondhand loot. Maximizing value is Sister Tesa's forte. Everything she wears and everything she lives with has been donated. Her stores also clothe all of the women and their children, including her thrift store manager Luz De Leon, who met Sister Tesa while serving ten years in Bedford Hills Correctional Facility for manslaughter.

"Tesa is a smart cookie," Luz confided to me in a conspiratorial tone. "She taught us all how to sell anything." She taught her well. Luz managed to sell me that sheared beaver cape the first time that we met.

Prisoners are released without any clothes. Sister Tesa's women don't have pajamas to sleep in or suits for interviews. "We have anything they need," Sister Tesa said gleefully, rummaging through the shelves of the shop. "We have sweaters and suits and coats. At any given time we have twenty strollers. And we have bling," she said with delight. "Everyone wants some bling." She pressed a sparkly necklace into my hands. "It's only five dollars. You should buy it."

Sister Tesa believes in both second chances and in the fact that most of the women she works with never deserved to be in prison in the first place. "If they just had better lawyers, they wouldn't have gone in. If they were the Lindsay Lohans of our life, things would have been different for them," she explained with a touch of derision in her voice, either for the system or for Ms. Lohan, the actress who has consistently been able to avoid serving jail time for her many felonies. Most of Sister Tesa's women got sent away for a drug-related crime or sometimes burglary, often committed to get money for drugs. She sees it all as bad timing and even worse circumstances.

"A lot of it is the drug culture. It can lead to such negative behavior. The women become targets. A lot of them didn't even use drugs. They were just in the wrong place at the wrong time, and then their entire family pays for it," Sister Tesa said with a shake of her head. "These are good women. They made mistakes, just like the rest of us."

Sister Tesa grew up poor in a working-class Irish family in the Five Towns of Nassau County out on Long Island. Her parents were Irish immigrants who made education and faith the cornerstones of their lives. Her mom was the gregarious one. She could make anyone laugh. Sister Tesa is more like her father—slightly reserved and introspective, yet witty and warm. She claims that she didn't have one singular moment when she knew she would be a sister. It was more of a long and drawn-out calling that has been with her as long as she can remember.

"It was this inner sense that this was a good thing for me to do. It wasn't an aha! moment, where I woke up and said, 'Hey I want to be a nun today.' It was just a constant calling from God." She didn't talk much about it with her family until she actually went off and joined the Sisters of St. Joseph, who'd taught her in both elementary and high school.

"Those women seemed so happy and they were doing good things, so it just made sense to me." Sister Tesa pulled a picture out of her drawer to show me. It is an old picture of her sitting on a park bench with her mother and father, taken in the '60s, the day she joined the order. Sister Tesa is wearing a full black-and-white habit. As a Vatican II sister, it was one of the only times she would ever wear the full habit. These days she is partial to perfectly pleated jeans, brightly colored sweaters, and smart blazers. In the photograph, her dad is gazing at her with a mixture of pride and concern.

Sister Tesa laughs. "I think he is just wondering, 'Is she happy?'" The answer was yes. She says she has been happy since the day she took her vows.

God is a constant in Sister Tesa's life. "God is in the fabric of my day. We walk together every minute of the day," she told me. She finds herself talking to God all the time. After she mentions it, I catch her, in the middle of regular conversation, taking a second to ask the Lord for something.

In 1986, Sister Tesa was living with other sisters in her order and working as the curriculum coordinator for the Brooklyn diocese. A friend, Sister Elaine Roulet, the director of the Children's Center at the Bedford Hills Correctional Facility, asked her to escort a young child to Rikers Island so that the child could visit her mother.

Sister Elaine is a legend in the world of prison reform. As recently as the 1980s, many women in prison had no way to see their children on a regular basis while they served time. It was she who established the precedent of connecting imprisoned moms with their babies.

It all began while Sister Elaine was teaching the women inmates of a maximum-security prison in New York how to read. The reading program was fine, the inmates told her, but could she help them with what they really wanted? They wanted to know where their kids were, what they were up to, and how they could communicate with them. Sister Elaine became something called a prison family liaison for the next ten years and answered those exact questions. Most prisons in our country still use the model she put in place to try to maintain some kind of continuity in a family while mothers are locked up. Sister Tesa's first trip with Sister Elaine took just over an hour and completely changed the trajectory of her life.

"I couldn't imagine what happened to children when their mother was taken from them," Sister Tesa told me. "So in retrospect, it was God's divine providence, because I was hooked."

Seeing firsthand the consequences of forced separation on a child was gut-wrenching. There was uncertainty and fear preparing for the visit, followed by separation anxiety and depression on the way back. It just wasn't right. Sisters Tesa and Elaine tried to work out a way to fix it.

Step one was to make sure that the children of inmates had a safe place to grow up while their moms were away. Could Sister Tesa take them in? God help her, she had no idea. When she became a nun, she gave up on the idea of ever being a mother, and she was happy with that decision. She prayed and meditated on the idea and ultimately knew the right thing to do. Sister Tesa and the other sisters, five of them in all, became foster mothers and committed to raising the children until their mothers were let out. They found a space in the Convent of St. Rita's on Twelfth Street in Long Island City. Volunteers, family, and friends all came to help clean it out and turn it into a place that was fit for kids to live and grow up in.

Their first charge was a fifteen-month-old little girl named Naté, who was born in prison and had never seen wide-open spaces until Sister Tesa brought her to Queens, both of them uncertain about what the next few months would hold. Three other kids came in the first year, including a little girl who arrived on October 31 with a suitcase and a Halloween costume.

They didn't want the children in their care to feel alienated from the other kids in the neighborhood or at school, so they named the building "My Mother's House." That way, when outsiders asked them where they were going back to, they never felt like it was lying. They said, "My Mother's House," and no one asked them any more questions. Sister Tesa became a licensed foster mother, which she quickly learned was a completely different job from taking care of the kids during the day as a teacher.

"It was a real eye-opener. I got a crash course in empathetic understanding of what parents go through," Sister Tesa told me. "It was hard. You had highs and lows. You had to let each child be an individual. The babies were actually easier to bond with. It was harder with the teenagers, who came in with all the baggage of life."

Candy drives, which she thought were such a great idea when she worked as a principal of a school in her earlier life, were particularly taxing. "When I saw these kids walk in with a hundred and twenty chocolate bars to sell, I wanted to choke." She remembers walking down the street with two-year-old Amelia, five-year-old Julia, and a wagon of chocolate. Julia would go on to become the top chocolate seller in her kindergarten class.

"It sure was a different model. We had five sisters raising the children and we did all the things a parent would do. I became a mom," Sister Tesa said. "But my commitment was to their mothers. Every weekend we would ride up to Bedford [Hills Correctional Facility] and take the babies to see their mothers. It was a ritual for nine years."

One little girl would sit in the back of the giant van explaining to her imaginary friend what it would be like in the prison. Sister Tesa drove and listened to the little girl chatter to the air about how excited she was for the visit. She would plunge into tremendous detail about how pretty her mother would look, what she would be wearing and what color lipstick she would have on. She talked all about what they would eat out of the vending machines and what kinds of crafts they would do.

That conversation made Sister Tesa wipe away tears as she drove. That right there. That was her goal, for the child to love and connect to a parent they could only see once a week. That is why it was imperative for her to step away once they got to the prison, to make sure the children had one-on-one time with their real moms. It was even more important for the younger ones, who tended to bond closely with the sisters.

On the drive back, they would debrief.

"We talked about what happened during the day, the highlights of the visit. The reflection was important," Sister Tesa told me. Having a parent in prison was a taboo topic of conversation in any other circumstance, but in that van the kids were all in the same boat. They could talk about how awesome it was, how scary, and how sad. They could admit that the prison smelled gross sometimes but their moms smelled good. They weren't afraid to cry in front of one another.

Leaving the prison was always the hard part.

"Until the kids got used to the idea that the visits wouldn't be erratic, they screamed and they cried. For the new ones it was always a readjustment. The ones who best prepared them were the other kids."

What Sister Tesa didn't expect was just how fun some of the trips could be.

The nun is partial to Christian music, but she learned all the top-forty songs from the 1980s and '90s by heart.

"I remember 'Walk Like an Egyptian' very vividly," she told me, belting out a couple of lines from the 1986 Bangles hit.

The entire process took a toll on Sister Tesa, too. It was never easy to give up the children when their mothers got out. Giving up Naté, that first baby, was particularly hard. Sister Tesa cried for an hour as she prepared to hand her back over to her mom. Julia, one of the other children, was just four years old then, but her words of wisdom were much older. She looked at Sister Tesa, distraught over Naté, and said to her very matter-of-factly, "This is the way it is supposed to be. But it's OK, you are allowed to cry."

It wasn't just the idea of relinquishing a child that rocked Sister Tesa; it was the pain of handing them over to an uncertain future. These children hadn't committed any crime.

"It became very clear to me that the mothers didn't have the opportunities that the children deserved," Sister Tesa said. She wanted something more for all of them. She knew that when these women were released, they would need the embrace of a supportive community, or post-prison pressures would break them—and likely their kids.

She was further inspired by Doreen, a woman she met in prison and whose son Hakeem she had taken in. Doreen had been a foster child herself when she became addicted to drugs as a teenager, and she was still very much a child by the time she was locked up. While in prison, she gave birth to Hakeem. Doreen completed drug treatment while serving her time, but she had no options once she was released. She had nowhere to live, no education, no skills, and no money.

When Sister Tesa first met her, Doreen was sobbing uncontrollably because she knew she would be homeless when she was released and that none of the state-run shelters would let her keep Hakeem with her. Sister Tesa tried to plead Doreen's case with the administration for the halfway houses. Their response was stern: "We have no room for mothers with their children." This was a common occurrence in New York state. Sister Tesa knew then that she had to find a space, not just for Doreen, but for all of the mothers.

They expanded St. Rita's to be able to accommodate the moms. These days, the women live in St. Rita's, as well as three other communal homes in Long Island City.

As mushy as she can be with the kids, Sister Tesa enforces the rules. Women are required to enroll in Hour Children's employment and training program. They must comply with sober and communal living restrictions and responsibilities. They ultimately need to get a job, and they have to keep finding ways to give back to the community.

If they meet these requirements, they are welcome to

stay for as long as they feel they need support. Some have stayed with Hour Children for a few months, others as long as fifteen years.

Only women are allowed to be on a lease in Sister Tesa's apartment buildings.

"It gives them control. It gives them the power to say no to the men in their lives," Sister Tesa said.

Hour Children's holdings in the neighborhood provide a microcosm of the real world. There is the food pantry, the source of food for the women when they first live on their own, and a huge boon for the rest of the neighborhood, which ranges from poor to working class. Local politicians love Hour Children's food pantry. The Twelfth District's congresswoman, Carolyn Maloney, hosted a press conference there when the Democrats were trying to pass the farm bill in 2013. There is a building for the Working Women Program, where the former inmates are taught life and career skills and prepped for internships and jobs all over Queens. Sister Tesa spent years convincing the Con Edison plant to take on her women as employees, and in 2013, they had eight Hour Children women in their intern training program. There is the day-care center where women can leave their kids while they go to their new jobs. "When you're taking in mothers and children, you have no choice but to provide child care," Sister Tesa told me with her typically intense certainty.

Sister Tesa's biggest achievement was the demolition of

the old Trinitarian convent across the street from St. Rita's. In 2013, she secured $9.4 million in funding to buy the property from the diocese, demolish it, and then reconstruct it from scratch. In its place she built an apartment building with eighteen renovated apartments for former inmates who need permanent housing.

The rent will never rise above one-third of a woman's income and averages around $500 for a two-bedroom apartment. There is plenty of room for their kids. Each apartment was beautifully furnished before the women moved in, the handiwork of longtime Hour Children volunteer and interior designer Connie Steinberg, who scoured Home Goods stores up and down the East Coast to make each apartment unique for the woman who would live there. Ms. Steinberg put tea towels in the bathrooms, patterned rugs on the floors, and brand-new mirrors in the hallways.

Each apartment came with a pair of fuzzy slippers for each family member; on the weekends, the women can hear the soft shuffle of their neighbors moving between floors.

Right before the apartments were ready for move-in, Sister Tesa took the women on a tour of their new homes. One former inmate, Venita Pinckney, a mother of two kids, just sat down on her new couch and cried.

"Is this really my new house?" she asked.

The nun nodded, then added, "You deserve it."

Ms. Pinckney, forty-two years old, spent a year and a half in Bedford Hills Correctional Facility for a drug crime before walking out in 2010. Her son, Savion, a five-year-old with a broad smile and a penchant for LEGOs, was born in the prison nursery. Today, Ms. Pinckney is a housing coordinator for Hour Children.

She shyly told Ms. Steinberg that she had always wanted to live in an apartment decorated in all black and white. The interior designer delivered.

"I never thought I would live somewhere so beautiful. My life was sure chaotic before I met Sister Tesa," Ms. Pinckney said as she cooked grits and bacon one Saturday morning. "When you out there on the street," she said, "you don't think someone like Sister Tesa could love a total stranger. I'm glad she loves me." Getting her new apartment helped Ms. Pinckney regain custody of her sixteen-year-old daughter, Janaye. "I got her back because I'm clean," she said, "and I have this apartment."

Sister Tesa has never met a bargain she doesn't love, and every other building she works in is filled with secondhand furniture. But it was important to her that, in this case, the women received nice new things.

"It says, 'We value you.' It helps them move forward and start a whole new life. They will take care of these things and they will feel special," Sister Tesa said as she gave me a tour of the new apartments.

Next door to the new apartment building is Theresa's Hair Salon, a full-service salon with three styling chairs that provides hair-cutting and -coloring, as well as makeup lessons. Rosa Peralta, a voluptuous and handsome woman in her forties with a bouffant of inky hair with crimson highlights, runs the salon. When Sister Tesa first met her at the Taconic Correctional Facility, Rosa was doing time for a drug sale and didn't speak a word of English. She has been working for the nun for fifteen years.

I asked Rosa what her life would have been like if she hadn't met Sister Tesa.

"I don't think about it," she told me without pause. "She gave me another chance. She gave me another family. She changed my entire life."

These women have changed Sister Tesa as much as she has changed them by inspiring her to have a grander vision for her own life.

"They look at their lives very honestly. They have a resiliency to admit their past and then create a vision for their future, and that is a lesson for us all," she told me. "They don't dwell in the negative. They have a vision for where they want to go, and the small steps they need to take to get there. I think about that all the time."

Sister Tesa operates with an enviable forward momentum. This brassy little nun will hustle for her women until the day she dies. We were saying good-bye one fall afternoon outside of St. Rita's when she looked across the street and lifted a finger to point at something over there. In between the hair salon and one of the thrift stores sat a two-story brick building with commercial space on the first floor and apartments on the second.

"We need to buy that," she said with conviction, before she looked past me and had one of her side conversations with God. "Lord, we can put women in apartments on the second floor and they can work in the Laundromat. That is what I want. I want to run a Laundromat filled with former felons. Lord, if you are listening, I want to run a Laundromat before I die."

9.

Jesus Treated Men and Women Equally

*Women's status in the Church is the
single most important and radical issue of our time.*

—Sister Maureen Fiedler

She was famished. Men, and even a few women, walked by Sister Maureen Fiedler in their well-pressed suits and polished loafers on their way to work, some taunting her by eating just a few inches in front of her face. The food—fruit, bagels, breakfast sandwiches—looked so tempting, but she refused to consume anything but water. Wearing a white robe with a regal purple sash, the colors of the early suffragists, Sister Maureen sat in protest with seven other women inside the Capitol rotunda in Springfield, Illinois, abstaining from food for the thirty-seven days in 1982 that the state legislature debated the Equal Rights Amendment.

"You're hungry for the first few days, but then your body adjusts," she explained to me, more than thirty years after her five-week hunger strike in the last northern state to hold out on ratifying the amendment that would provide women with rights equal to men. "I began to understand what it means that prayer and fasting go together, because being hungry draws you to prayer in a different way. At some point you just stop concentrating on your own needs and start concentrating on something larger. So the idea of prayer comes more naturally to you," she told me as I bit into a medium-rare burger over lunch at a greasy spoon called Plato's Diner, across the street from her office in College Park, Maryland. I nodded, feeling a small pang of guilt for never having a moment that inspired me to put my own needs aside for that kind of cause.

Sister Maureen's hope as she fasted in the rotunda for weeks on end was that the ERA would change things for all women, and that its passage could help influence the Catholic Church's antiquated rules against women being leaders.

She and her fellow protestors were mindful of their health, drinking plenty of water and meeting with a doctor to monitor their vitals.

"We were very careful not to kill ourselves," Sister Maureen told me in her pragmatic way.

It was still dangerous stuff. One woman was briefly hospitalized, and even Sister Maureen was taken to the emergency room at one point to have an EKG. But on June 23 it became clear that they would not receive the 60 percent of the vote necessary for ratification. Sister Maureen sipped on grape juice for the first time in over a month. Spectators applauded their efforts, but the ERA was tabled across the country.

Maureen Fiedler was born in Lockport, New York, on October 31, 1942—Halloween.

"I won't even get into the number of jokes that has inspired over the years," she told me. "To this day, I am spooking people." Her parents were Catholic, but not the strict kind.

At around age eight or nine, Maureen was watching her mom iron clothes and wondered, "Is this my future?" She couldn't imagine anything more boring than a lifetime of household chores.

Role-playing Mass in her living room, Maureen was the priest and her younger brother, Mike, was the altar boy. It was a few years still until she realized being a priest wasn't a thing that was possible for her in real life.

Maureen's father was an early feminist who wouldn't have dared allow anyone to call him that. In the 1950s he encouraged his daughter to take the kinds of classes typically set aside for the boy children—physics, chemistry, biology, and trigonometry. When Maureen told her dad that she might want to be a nurse, he countered, "Why wouldn't you be a doctor?"

In high school she started thinking about becoming a nun, but Maureen wasn't particularly attracted to the nuns teaching at her school, the Sisters of St. Mary de Namur. In her sophomore year, her high school, St. Joseph's Academy, merged with De Sales High School, a boys' school. By her senior year, Maureen's grades were so good that she was the valedictorian. The principal, a priest, told her she couldn't give the valedictory address because she was a girl. She went home and talked to her mother about it. "Don't get into a fight with a priest," her mother warned.

"This is wrong. I have earned this," Maureen thought.

"I had to stand up to it," she told me. And so the headstrong girl marched into the principal's office and told him what he was doing was unjust and that it would look absolutely terrible on the front page of the local newspaper. She planned to publicize the incident and tell the paper if he did not change his mind.

"I knew the power of publicity even then," she said, smiling at me, her red dangly earrings waving back and forth in a silent cheer for her younger self.

She gave the valedictory speech.

"For me, that was a seminal moment in my life, when I actually experienced that kind of discrimination," she told me.

The sisters at Mercyhurst College in Erie, Pennsylvania, were a different story from the nuns in high school. They were inspiring intellectuals, and before long, Maureen felt a serious call to the sisterhood.

"I don't know how to describe it," she said. "It came to me in prayer and I couldn't shake it, no matter how hard I tried."

She was just nineteen years old when she moved into the convent, and her parents were livid. They didn't come to see her for a year after she'd left home.

"My mother didn't want me to do it at all. She wanted me to settle down and get married and have children, and I didn't see that in my future."

She entered the novitiate just as Vatican II was commencing in 1962. Sister Maureen and her fellow novices hungrily consumed all of the documents the Vatican released. Access to news outside the novitiate was limited, but Sister Maureen couldn't help but learn about a Baptist preacher down South named Martin Luther King Jr., who was also fighting for social justice. The connection between what the Church was asking and what the civil rights movement was doing became very clear in her mind.

"I wanted to go to Selma. Of course, I was barely wet

behind the veil, so I got a no when I asked," Sister Maureen told me. The rules were still so strict that the young nun wasn't even permitted to attend a sympathy march for Selma in downtown Erie, just a mile from the convent.

Soon after, she moved to Pittsburgh and began to make friends with members of the local NAACP. When Dr. King was assassinated in 1968, Pittsburgh was a powder keg. The Hill District, then the city's largest ghetto, erupted in flames. At the time Sister Maureen was teaching social studies and religion at a predominantly white inner-city school, where racism thrived. She decided she could do some good by taking her privileged white students to tutor the black kids over in the Hill District. She still had the problem of having to sign out and be accounted for by her convent whenever she wasn't teaching.

"I quickly learned that signing out could be as vague as vague can be, so I just signed out for 'town.' Most people thought I was shopping. I wasn't shopping."

Sister Maureen recalls fondly the day one of her white students came to her with his arm slung around a young black student and asked permission to walk to town to buy the poorly shod younger boy shoes with his own money. It made her feel a very real sense of accomplishment in her work.

Her thirst for social justice grew stronger, and in the fall of 1970, Sister Maureen headed to Georgetown University to pursue her master's in political science. She was raised to be unfailingly patriotic, but at Georgetown she found herself on the side of the anti–Vietnam War activists. She went on to get her PhD with a dissertation asking why women were not elected political leaders in the same numbers as men, despite the second wave of American feminism.

While in Washington, she searched for a spiritual director. A friend at a new group called NETWORK suggested a Jesuit priest named William Callahan. He had launched a group called Priests for Equality, calling for the equality of women with men in all walks of life, including the priesthood. In 1976, Callahan co-founded (with Dolly Pomerleau) the Quixote Center, a social justice institution where, as he put it, "people could dream impossible dreams of justice and make them come true." Sister Maureen would spend the next thirty years there.

Women's ordination in the Catholic Church is one of the often-overlooked feminist issues from the 1970s, perhaps because organizers never succeeded in accomplishing their goal. That most certainly wasn't due to lack of trying.

Accompanied by Callahan, who was scheduled to speak at the conference, and Pomerleau, Sister Maureen attended the first national Women's Ordination Conference in Detroit on Thanksgiving weekend of 1975. The conference was the brainchild of a Catholic feminist named Mary B. Lynch, who felt compelled, in the winter of 1974, to ask all of the people on her Christmas list whether they thought it was high time that Catholic women were allowed to become priests. Thirty-one women and one man responded with a resounding yes. Soon after, she set out to organize a conference that would work to build a case for women in the priesthood. She expected a small group of like-minded women to meet her in Detroit. Instead, more than two thousand Catholic women flooded into the city for the meeting.

Women priests seemed like a real possibility after Vatican II. In those heady early days of change and social activism, it truly seemed like anything could happen in the Church. Talking about it today, Sister Maureen can still quote with authority from the section of the Vatican's edict on the Church and the modern world. "Any type of social or cultural discrimination based on sex is to be overcome and eradicated as contrary to God's intent . . . it is deeply to be deplored that these basic personal rights are not yet being respected everywhere, as is the case with women who are denied the chance freely to choose a husband or a state of life."

At the Michigan conference, speakers espoused the position that it was a moral imperative that women should be equals of men in the priesthood. Sister of Notre Dame Marie Augusta Neal stood up to proclaim, "God has no pronouns." Sister of Mercy Elizabeth Carroll riffed on the many meanings of the phrase "the proper place of women in the Church," and scripture scholars Elisabeth Schüssler

Fiorenza and Fr. Carroll Stuhlmueller set out to prove that the Bible never explicitly says that women cannot be priests. The pièce de résistance came at the end of the conference, when an organizer asked for every woman who felt called to the priesthood to stand to be blessed. Hundreds of women stood tall. Sister Maureen didn't.

"I don't advocate for women priests because I want to be a priest," she told me. "I don't have any desire to become a priest. But I want to be a catalyst to make it possible."

Women becoming church leaders wasn't unattainable in other faith traditions at the time. Other religions had already embraced equality wholeheartedly. In 1972, the Jewish Reform movement ordained Sally J. Priesand as America's first female rabbi. In 1974, the "Philadelphia Eleven" caused a firestorm within the Episcopal Church when eleven female deacons presented themselves to three male bishops to be ordained as priests. In the Roman Catholic Church, women couldn't even be ordained as deacons, much less priests or bishops. Sister Maureen didn't accept that. To her, Jesus was, and is, an "equal-opportunity employer." He loved everyone the same.

"It was probably male scribes that wrote most of the Gospels, since women back then couldn't read, but I do not think the women in those stories got a fair shake," Sister Maureen says, citing the story of the Last Supper as proof. The Gospels are often interpreted as saying Jesus ordained all of the men who attended the Last Supper.

"But we don't have a guest list for the upper room." She went on: "Who *cooked* that dinner? I don't imagine it was the Apostles. There were undoubtedly women there, and I suspect that they were—like the men—in earshot when he said, 'Do this in remembrance of me.'"

Then there is preaching the resurrection. The first person whom Jesus encountered after he rose from the dead was Mary Magdalene, and it was she whom he commissioned to preach the resurrection. "Only then did she run off and get the boys," Sister Maureen said.

"The problem is that those Gospels are written in a way that doesn't give women enough credit. I actually think that in the early Church—and by that, I mean the first century or two—women were close to being the equals of men. I think it is one of the suppressed realities in Church history."

Some of those stories still exist, mostly about wealthy women. There was Olympias, a patroness of three of the bishops of Constantinople in the early fifth century. When she was widowed at age thirty, Bishop Nectarius ordained her as a deacon, in no small part because he wanted her large fortune for the Church. There are first-century frescoes that some scholars believe depict women giving out communion or being ordained.

Sister Maureen was exhilarated by the Detroit conference, afterward becoming a full-fledged member of the Women's Ordination Conference. She began a polling project to determine how other Catholics felt about the woman-priest issue. She coauthored, with Dolly Pomerleau, the publication of the results: a report entitled "Are Catholics Ready?"

"As feminists, we are aware of the Church officials' claims that the Catholic people are not ready for full equality. We realize, however, that these claims are based on a combination of old and scanty data, mixed with speculation. But we also recognize that the claims raise important questions that must be answered with hard, new, sociological data if public discussion of the issues is to be informed," she wrote in the introduction to the study. The poll concluded that Vatican II Catholics—the more progressive members of the Church, the ones who wanted their Mass in English—were receptive to the idea of women priests.

Rome wasn't having it. In January 1977, the Vatican Congregation for the Doctrine of the Faith delivered a decisive no on the question of women priests. Their calculus was that because Jesus Christ was a man, women couldn't be ordained in his image. "The Catholic Church has never felt that priestly or episcopal ordination can be validly conferred on women . . . by calling only men to the priestly order and ministry in its true sense, the Church intends to remain faithful to the type of ordained ministry willed by the Lord Jesus Christ and carefully maintained by the Apostles," they wrote.

The American bishops considered the issue settled. The nuns, and a lot of other Catholic women, did not.

In 1977, Sister Maureen cast a wider net for women's rights, co-founding the organization Catholics Act for ERA. The ERA was a simple amendment with tremendous consequences that would add a single line to the United States Constitution: "Equality of rights under the law shall not be denied or abridged by the United States or by any State on account of sex." Lobbyists spent the next ten years trying to ratify the amendment in the required thirty-eight states. For four years, Sister Maureen lobbied in Illinois, Oklahoma, Nevada, Missouri, and Florida in favor of it, meeting all the major players in the feminist movement, Ellie Smeal, then the President of the National Organization for Women (NOW), as well as Molly Yard and Patricia Ireland, who would both go on to lead NOW. She learned to fund raise and became a seasoned speaker on the issue of women's rights, ready to give a stump speech in front of three thousand people at a moment's notice.

When Pope John Paul II made his first visit to the United States in October 1979, Sister Maureen helped to organize the "Stand Up for Women" demonstration at the Shrine of the Immaculate Conception in Washington, DC, where fifty-three Catholic sisters wore blue armbands and refused to sit down during the pope's speech in order to call attention to the lack of gender equality in the Catholic Church.

"We stand in solidarity with all women out of love and concern for the Church, to call the Church to repentance for the injustice of sexism, because we believe the Church can change," read a statement distributed at the event.

At the same event, Sister Theresa Kane, president of the Leadership Conference of Women Religious, representing most of the nation's 140,000 nuns, stood up to the podium wearing a brown suit and a jaunty checkered blouse with a bow at the neck. The pope cocked his head, poised to listen, forming a wide steeple with his fingers in front of his face. Sister Theresa took a deep breath before asking the pope for equality for women. "The Church in its struggle to be faithful to its call for reverence and dignity for all persons must respond by providing the possibility of women as persons being included in all ministries of our Church," she said, growing more confident with each word. "I urge you, Your Holiness, to respond to the voices coming from the women of this country who are desirous of serving in and with this Church as fully participating members." It may have been the only moment that a sister would have been able to confront the pope on an issue like this. The pope was taken aback.

"You know, I was looking at him that day," Sister Maureen later said with a laugh in an interview with NPR in her warm but frank way. "And it didn't look like he had a smile on his face. He seemed like he was thinking, 'Oh my, nobody vetted this speech, did they?'"

Nuns began leaving their communities in droves in the late '60s, '70s, and '80s, as more and more opportunities opened up to women who lived outside of convents. The leader of Sister Maureen's order in Erie vacated her post to marry a former priest and was replaced by a conservative sister who still wore a habit.

"It didn't look promising for nuns like me who were out there fasting for the ERA," Sister Maureen told me. "A friend—Dolly Pomerleau—said to me, 'You are a nun at heart. You can't just leave your community.' Mind you, she had left hers."

Sister Maureen sent résumés to ten orders, looking for a family that would embrace her dedication to social justice. Only two sent back a personal response: the Sisters of St. Joseph, home to Helen Prejean, whose work with convicted murderers would eventually be turned into a memoir and an Academy Award–winning movie (*Dead Man Walking*), and the Sisters of Loretto, known in progressive circles as the social justice nuns. She opted for Loretto and has never looked back.

Meanwhile, Sister Maureen was working as a co-director of the justice-oriented Quixote Center. In the 1980s, she spent several years organizing and lobbying against the Reagan administration's wars in Central America. She was part of the Quest for Peace Project, which organized massive amounts of humanitarian aid for the people of Nicaragua who were victims of war—even matching the amount of aid that Congress had approved for the US-supported "contras."

At times, she joined in acts of civil disobedience to protest US policy. "The worst thing I did, I guess, was join others to pray in the Capitol rotunda. That earned me five days in the DC jail."

As the new millennium approached, Sister Maureen found a new calling. In the late 1980s, she was commuting home to care for both of her dying parents. During those long drives between DC and western New York, mostly through rural Pennsylvania, she had nothing to keep her awake but fundamentalist Christian radio.

"I would get furious when I listened to it. It wasn't Christian as I understood 'Christian.' It was anti-woman. It was anti-gay. It never talked about peace." This was the way people heard about religion, through the radio, through a lens of intolerance.

"I thought I could create an alternative."

There is no doubt about it: Sister Maureen's voice was made for public radio. Her tone is measured and soothing, her humor dry. She hits her marks. One Sunday afternoon, she put me on speakerphone during one of our talks so she could tidy up and prepare to put her chicken dinner in the oven while we spoke.

At one point the toilet flushed.

"It's not what you think," Sister Maureen said, explaining that one of her three cats had "deposited his poop in an inconvenient place and I got rid of it." She is a straight shooter, whether she's talking about the Islamic tensions underlying the Arab Spring or one of her cats, Napoleon: Conqueror of All He Surveys. Napoleon, a longhaired tuxedo, was born right in her bed. Sister Maureen had no idea that his mother, Cleopatra, Queen of the Nile, was pregnant when she took her in, but she woke up one morning to find Cleopatra licking off three newborn kittens. The third cat is a tough guy—Einstein, the Three-Legged Genius.

Sister Maureen began doing commentaries with NPR in the late '90s and started a commercial call-in show called *Faith Matters*, which had a short shelf life from 1999 to 2001. Then 9/11 happened. The Saturday after the terrorist attacks on New York City and Washington, DC, Sister Maureen felt called to round up a group of interfaith guests for a three-hour special called "Religion & Terrorism."

They had five phone lines ringing at once and there wasn't a quiet line all night. *Interfaith Voices* was born—a radio show with the mission of bringing together disparate religious voices. Today the show airs in seventy-four markets and counting. Its mission is public education in the full spectrum of major religious traditions and a mandate to confront anything that even vaguely smells like discrimination.

When the Vatican began its Apostolic Visitation, or investigation of American nuns, in 2009, Sister Maureen was able to use her platform to defend the sisters on air and her position as a commentator to speak out.

She wrote an op-ed for *Ms.* magazine:

Most progressive nuns suspect a desire by the church hier-
archy to rein in the independent lifestyles and ministries of
active, often outspoken, feminist women, and to push them
back into highly scheduled convent living and recogniz-
able religious garb (habits). Other nuns see the investiga-
tions as an attempt to silence their cries against injustices
in the church. Fueling such suspicions are the three tar-
gets of the doctrinal investigation: It will assess whether
nuns' leaders accept the all-male priesthood, adhere to
church teaching that homosexual activity is "intrinsically
disordered," and believe that only the Catholic Church
provides salvation, while other Christian churches have
"defects." Those teachings have been challenged for years
by prominent theologians. Many nuns have been active
for decades in the movement for women's ordination to the
priesthood. Some nuns have questioned teachings on con-
traception and abortion. Others have defended the rights
of gays and lesbians, and still others work for interfaith
understanding and collaboration.

She also took to the *Huffington Post*:

Some [nuns] participate in anti-war and anti-torture cam-
paigns and demonstrations, or protest at the School of the

223

Americas in Georgia. Not a few have gone to jail. Many work with the poor and advocate for the poor in legislatures. And many work with poor women specifically—in homeless shelters, rape crisis centers and centers that deal with domestic violence. Some commentators think that [Cardinal Franc] Rodé and his ilk wanted to put an end to all of this and return American nuns to the classroom and convent. As a nun who has long been involved in peace and justice work, interfaith collaboration and the rights of women, there is virtually no chance of that happening.

In 2010, Sister Maureen published the book *Breaking Through the Stained Glass Ceiling*, a series of interviews she conducted on *Interfaith Voices* dealing with discrimination faced by women in all religions and the emerging leadership of women in some faith traditions.

"I say in the book, you know, in a day and age when Nancy Pelosi is the Speaker of the House of Representatives, when Hillary Clinton could be a credible candidate for president of the United States, being a woman bishop doesn't look like such a big deal anymore," Sister Maureen told NPR in 2011. Her interviews in the book, which also aired on the radio show, include talks with Bishop Katharine Jefferts Schori, the first woman presiding bishop of the Episcopal Church and the first woman primate of the Anglican Communion; Dr. Ingrid Mattson, the first woman president of the Islamic Society of North America;

and Rev. Susan Andrews, the first woman National Moderator of the Presbyterian Church.

Plenty of Sister Maureen's fellow sisters have left the Church for religious organizations where the stained-glass ceiling has already been broken, or for completely new callings that don't restrict them based on gender. Sister Maureen herself has no plans to leave.

She believes that being a champion for women's rights is easier to do from within the Catholic Church. "I see it as a part of my calling. And I think a lot of women of faith would say the same thing," Sister Maureen told me. "My vow of obedience is a vow of obedience to the call of God and to the call of Jesus. And first among that is to do justice."

Sister Maureen is busy. She is hosting the radio show, she is writing books, she is penning op-eds and appearing as a commentator on other people's shows. She loves dogs but she is too busy to own one; that is why she has her three cats. But when she jogs, which she tries to do every day to keep both her mind and body fit, she takes dog treats with her in her pockets so that she has an excuse to pet the neighborhood canines. One day, she introduced herself to one of the dogs' owners.

"Oh my," the woman exclaimed. "You're that woman on the radio!" Sister Maureen is a little bit famous in certain circles.

With so much focus at the end of 2013 on whether the newly elected Pope Francis could change the Church for minorities, including women, Sister Maureen became a valued commentator for various media outlets. "I really like Pope Francis in so many ways. He seems personable, friendly, truly human, a man who experiences life with joy. I love his simpler lifestyle, his emphasis on the poor of the world and his preaching of social justice and peace as cornerstones of the Gospel message," Sister Maureen wrote for the *National Catholic Reporter* in November of 2013. "But when it comes to women, I want to cry. He just doesn't seem to get it. He tries to be nice, to be complimentary and understanding. But in almost every phrase, he seems to think of women as a different species of human."

Sister Maureen doesn't think that Pope Francis will be the pope to finally ordain women. Only nine months into his tenure, she just didn't think he has it in him. She could hear it in his language, in the words he uses to describe women.

"He talks about women's sensitivity and intuition. He says women are sentimental and empathetic. He says women are socialized into these roles. He talks about loving motherhood. These are all positive stereotypes, but they are stereotypes nonetheless. He doesn't talk about women's intellect or their organizing ability or their political savvy," Sister Maureen said. "That's why I wish I could give him 'Women 101.'"

Even if the pope agreed to sit down and meet with feminist Catholic women like Sister Maureen, he would have to contend with all the men beneath him if he wanted to make real changes in how the Church deals with women.

"I doubt that he will move to ordain women, mainly because there will be a major revolt in the Vatican Curia," she said. "It is so male-entrenched there that the thought of having a bunch of powerful women around probably scares the living daylights out of them.

"But change will come," she says. "After all, Jesus was a feminist, and we claim to follow him."

10.

We Are All Sisters

A woman cannot have real autonomy unless she has reproductive autonomy. My hope is that one day both Church and society will embrace this justice issue.

—*Donna Quinn*

Donna Quinn doesn't like putting "Sister" in front of her name.

"We're all sisters," she says with a little bit of attitude. She prefers that people just call her Donna.

The protestors outside of a women's health clinic that performed abortions in Hinsdale, Illinois, didn't know that. To get her attention, they shouted at her.

"Sister, Sister!" they yelled as she peacefully walked

women from their cars and into the clinic. "Clinic Escort" was written across the front of her stark white smock, but again, she prefers another term—"peacekeeper."

The crowd of irate protestors alternated between praying the Rosary and ranting at the top of their lungs at the patients, mostly young girls who were exhausted as they tried to cross through the irritated crowd just to reach the front door of the simple one-story brick clinic on a tree-lined residential block. "They never questioned getting up at four a.m. to lurk outside of a women's health clinic, to attack a woman for being a moral agent in her own life. Who does that?" Donna asked me.

"Murderer!" the mob collectively shouted as one woman tried to pass. To Donna, the women's decision was a sacred one "made as a moral agent in a country that has said abortion is legal."

It is an incredible thing to walk with a woman, a stranger, as she heads into a clinic and prepares to undergo a surgery laden with moral, ethical, and psychological implications that will likely be with her for the rest of her life. In those moments Donna Quinn served as their protector and confidante. As she tried to walk with and shield those young women from further offense, she reminded herself that her work as a feminist activist was driven by a desire to leave this world a better place for subsequent generations.

"I wanted to be so much more than an escort. I wanted to be their human shield. These women put themselves in a vulnerable position because they made the right choice for themselves at the right time in their lives. I just wanted to put my arms around them and protect them," Donna told me. Many times that is exactly what she did, wrapping them in her thin arms and whispering words of comfort in their ears.

Donna Quinn has studied and spoken out on issues of reproductive justice for more than three decades and believes that a woman's right to make reproductive decisions for her own body should be safe, legal, accessible, and one day funded by Medicare.

"Any woman should have the right to choose an abortion," Donna said. "Just as men continue to make decisions for vasectomies and male-enhancing drugs, so too women should be able to make decisions for their bodies without jeering, name-calling, and violence as they enter health clinics for reasons unknown to those who perpetrate this violence on them because they are women. As a peacekeeper, my goal is to enable women to enter a health clinic for whatever reason in dignity and without fear of being physically assaulted."

After she became well known as a clinic escort, antichoice blogs started calling Donna the "Abortion Nun." The protestors had run the license plate of her car and figured out she was a Catholic sister.

When the stories took on a life of their own, Donna was asked by the leadership of her community to explain her work. The *Chicago Tribune* reported that she had decided to stop her work volunteering because the irate focus on her was escalating and she was worried that the safety of the women at the clinic could be put in jeopardy. "I want to be clear that this is my decision," she said. "Respect for a woman's moral agency is of critical importance to me and I look forward to continuing this dialogue with our congregation on these matters."

When it comes to abortion, Donna is at odds with the Vatican. The Catholic Church has changed its position on abortion throughout the centuries, but it currently takes the stance that human life must be protected absolutely from the moment of conception.

Still, every time we spoke, Donna Quinn told me, "I'm so Catholic."

Raised by a fearless mother and a generous father in the staunchly Irish Catholic parish of St. Gabriel in the Canaryville section of Chicago, Donna quickly learned that dedication to the Church was a way of life. Both parents were active in parish life. If her dad could have gotten up on the pulpit and delivered the sermon himself, he would have. Instead he would stand in the back of the church and motion to the priest when his sermon was going a little too long. He practically ran the parish, making sure that those with less got food, clothing, and shelter. Donna's mother took her own risks to help those in need, surreptitiously turning on the fire hydrant pump on their block so all the kids could cool off on hot summer days. Donna says that everything she now knows and practices about social justice, she learned from her family.

No one was surprised when all three Quinn siblings entered religious life. Early on, at the age of six, Donna's uncle asked her if she wanted to be a nun when she grew up. Not familiar with the word, she shook her head and replied, "No, I want to be a sister." When Donna was in the seventh grade, one of the order priests came to her school to try to sell the boys on the vocation. At the end of his talk, he asked the class who wanted to be ordained as a priest. Donna's hand shot up. The boys laughed and the priest informed her: "Oh no, only boys can become priests."

The sisters Donna had in high school were strong women, articulate and educated. Many of her classmates wanted to be teachers, nurses, secretaries, or homemakers, but she knew she wanted to be a nun. After earning degrees in administration and history, she taught grade school, high school, and college for seventeen years. Then, starting in the early 1970s, Donna became interested in the women's movement that was percolating on the heels of the previous decade's civil rights movement. She set off to take a closer look at where the Catholic Church stood on women's rights and was disappointed with what she learned. "After I took a look, I just realized that women essentially have no rights in the Catholic Church," she said. "And then I realized women have no voice, either."

One of the best things about being a nun in the 1970s, before the advent of e-mail, Twitter, and Facebook, was the ability to network. If you told a nun in San Francisco something, you could bet it would get to the Chicago sisters by the end of the week—through a flurry of letter writing, phone calls, and in-person visits. And so, in her thirties, Donna began focusing on bringing together nuns and other Catholic women to champion women's rights within the Church. She helped to found Chicago Catholic Women, the Women's Ordination Conference, and a coalition of twenty-six Catholic-rooted organizations known as Women-Church Convergence. She became one of the first members of the National Coalition of American Nuns (NCAN), a progressive group of sisters dedicated to studying and speaking out on justice issues in the Church and in society.

In the '70s she helped pull together a group called Women of the Church Coalition, consisting of about fifteen organizations springing up across the country that focused on women's issues in the Church.

The all-male National Conference of Catholic Bishops (NCCB) would meet every spring at the Palmer House in Chicago. The Coalition, thinking that they might leaflet and speak with bishops about women's issues, rented themselves a room and invited the bishops to join them for a lively discussion on women and the Church.

Donna thought it would be that easy. She thought they could just ask and they would receive. She now knows that she was incredibly naïve. "Oh, we were so filled with hope," she told me. Out of three hundred bishops, only two met with the women—Bishop Charles Buswell and Bishop Raymond Lucker.

"We thought all we had to do was be there and they would talk to us." Back then, the bishops did have a women's committee—a group where the men ostensibly gathered to discuss women. The chairman of that committee was a bishop named Michael Francis McAuliffe from Jefferson City, Missouri. He was on his way to the airport when Donna and two other women, Rosalie Muschal Reinhardt and Dolores Brooks, stopped him to ask if he and his fellow bishops might be interested in feminist theology classes and workshops on women's issues in the Church.

He released a buoyant belly laugh.

"I was amazed," Donna said. "He told me these men would never take a class from us. He wasn't mean-spirited. He just couldn't believe it. What I said was just so ludicrous to him."

The next year, the NCCB rented every room at the Palmer House, so the women took their leafleting to the streets outside and handed them out to people passing by.

"We were slowly learning that what we thought might take a few years to change might take a lifetime," Donna told me.

Abortion wasn't always Donna's first priority. Women's ordination was her first battle, followed by gaining rights for lesbian and gay Catholic members of the Church. She spent years focusing on advocacy for those issues through her work with NCAN.

In early 1984, Donna received a call from her friend Dolly Pomerleau of the Quixote Center in Washington, DC.

"Are you going to sign the ad calling for the bishops to dialogue on the issue of abortion?" Dolly asked at the end of their call. When I mentioned this call to Dolly twenty years later, she laughed and told me she didn't even remember the conversation. "But I probably said it," she said. The "call for dialogue" was a letter from the group Catholics for Free Choice (CFFC) that would be published in the *New York Times*, asking for a discussion of the Catholic position on abortion. The way CFFC saw it, there could be more than one stance on the morality of abortion, and those other stances were worth exploring. The letter was originally borne of a 1982 briefing that CFFC wrote for Congress detailing the difficulty of having a nuanced position on abortion for Catholic politicians. Then-Congresswoman Geraldine Ferraro penned the introduction for the briefing. When Ferraro was named Walter Mondale's running mate, Archbishop John O'Connor of New York and Archbishop Bernard Francis Law of Boston both issued statements denouncing her position on abortion.

The CFFC wanted to stand behind Ferraro. They turned the briefing into a letter arguing for a dialogue on the Catholic stance on abortion and looked for signatures from progressive Catholic leaders.

"All right, all right. I'll sign it," Donna replied. But she wanted to make it very clear: "This was not my first issue. This was not the issue I wanted to go down on."

A total of ninety-seven signatures were gathered, including Donna's, along with twenty-five other nuns and two priests. The CFFC paid $30,000 for the full-page ad in the *New York Times* that ran on the day many Catholic Americans celebrated "Respect for Life Sunday."

Weeks after the election, the US Conference of Catholic Bishops issued a statement saying that the opinions of the signers did not reflect those of the Church at large because they were in clear contradiction to the stance that a deliberately chosen abortion is objectively immoral. Cardinal Jean Jérôme Hamer, a Belgian Dominican, requested that the signers publicly retract their statements or be dismissed from their religious communities.

The following month, Cardinal Hamer came to Chicago to greet the religious men and women in the archdiocese. A large group gathered at the Holy Name Cathedral and after his speech everyone present was invited to the auditorium to personally meet the cardinal. Outside the cathedral, protestors gathered wearing black armbands to signify that the Church was dead to women. Many held signs reading, WE WANT A CHURCH FOR OUR DAUGHTERS.

Donna was the only signer of the ad inside the cathedral that day. She waited her turn in the long line to introduce herself to Cardinal Hamer and refused to take off her black armband. As she approached him, a woman protestor snapped a picture. As the camera's bright light went off, the cardinal went into a rage. He left Donna and chased the woman out of the building. When he returned, he was towering over the small nun.

She introduced herself. Cardinal Hamer accused Donna of organizing the protest. She dismissed that. What she wanted to ask him, since he, too, was of the Dominican order, was how might he help women and children in the shelter where she had a job-training program for women. She got as far as the word "Dominican" when he shouted at her, "You are not a good Dominican!"

She felt dizzy knowing this was a man of Rome . . . a man of the Vatican . . . a man of the Church to which she had given her life, who was angry with her. As black dots appeared before her eyes, she prayed she wouldn't faint at his feet. She mustered all of her courage to ask him if he would just take a meeting with the signers of the ad. Enraged, he replied, "You come to Rome . . . I will give you a meeting."

Donna went away with a determination to help women with reproductive issues from that day forward. "A woman cannot have real autonomy unless she has reproductive autonomy," she told me.

Donna is ripe with ideas.

Ask her what she thinks about the new pope and she quickly responds, "How many women were on the ballot? How many women voted for this pope or ever vote for the leadership in the Church? Women must be given the right to vote in the Church."

When the Vatican held their election conclave following the death of Pope John Paul II in 2005, Donna was furious with the fact that women weren't involved in the voting process.

"There is all of this talk about the gray smoke and the white smoke, and I started thinking, We need some pink smoke." She wondered about starting a campaign of burning pink smoke around the country to underscore the point that women had been left out of the conclave. Pink smoke, Donna soon learned, isn't so easy to come by.

"I thought all you would have to do is have incense burners and throw a pink or a red piece of material on top and it would send up pink smoke," she said. "There is something lacking in my science background, because I found out that you still get black or gray smoke." A brother of a friend of a friend had an Army job down in West Virginia. He was able to get Donna pellets that, when burned, could produce smoke of almost any color. Purple was the closest to pink in the bunch. Donna and the Women's Ordination Conference crossed the country for prayer vigils at cathedrals, sending up the purple-pink smoke at every stop.

"I just wanted to show people the lack of women in the election process. The intent was to signify that it ain't white or gray smoke, it is pink smoke that we need. I don't think most people understand the significance of the fact that women have no right to vote in the Catholic Church. The institutional Church has put us down and tried to keep us down. The Church is one of the biggest institutions in the world, and they are probably the most notorious for putting women down and not giving us our full rights."

Donna now sees ordination as part of a hierarchical system.

"Ordination was just something created centuries ago by men looking for power and looking for a way to keep women out of it. When we started the Women's Ordination Conference in 1975, we said we would create a new priestly ministry. We didn't just want to put women in vestments and zap us into something. It would be a whole new way of ministry. The ordination thing . . . just isn't needed. What we need is a whole new sacramental system, one where a man doesn't need to be present for the seven sacraments."

For inspiration, she looks to the Eucharist, or the practice of spirituality in everyday life.

"I am a Eucharistic person. I see the Eucharist in everything." I asked her to clarify what exactly she meant. "I am inspired by God and I see God in the people that I walk with. That is what Holy Communion means to me, that compassion between two people," she told me. "It is about being present."

Donna no longer stands outside abortion clinics, but she promises to keep up the fight for women's rights through political organizing and lobbying. She will go down shouting about what she believes is right.

"This is my issue," she told me. "I would die for this issue."

When Donna Quinn dies, she wants two things: a microphone in her casket and for people to remember her fight for women.

"We need a new sacramental system that tells the stories of women—stories our children will be proud to pass on to their next generations . . . stories told with pride by women, about women," Donna told me. "That is what we need, because we are all sisters."

Epilogue

Never let a nun get a pass at editing your book. As a journalist, I rarely let my subjects look at, much less touch, the stories I have written about them. But there was something about the nuns that made me feel like they deserved more than a fair shake when it came to how their lives would be presented to you, the reader. Maybe I felt that way because it seemed to me, after writing this book, that no one else was giving them their due. Maybe I'm not as agnostic as I like to believe and thought crossing the nuns would somehow lead to bad karma or a first-class ticket straight to hell. So, for whatever reason, I did let the sisters see bits and pieces of this book before it went to press. Most of them really enjoyed their chapters. One or two of them asked that I remove an offensive word or two. A couple of them spent days on end on the phone with me discussing how they were portrayed. In the end I did not make any major changes to this text. I was reminded that many of these women spent decades teaching grammar to schoolchildren. With their revisions, I have never handed over such clean copy to my publisher.

As I came to the end of my two-year journey with the nuns, people kept asking me what they saw as the obvious questions. There is the sarcastic one: *Are you going to run off and join a convent now?* No. That is usually followed by more serious ones: *Do you feel holier? Are you a Catholic now?*

The answer to both is no. I am still an agnostic who reads the *New York Times* on Sundays instead of going to church. But the book did inspire a kind of spiritual shift in me. The question I wish that people would ask me is *How have the nuns changed you?* The answer to that is quite a lot, actually.

These days, I often find myself thinking, What would the nuns do?

When I get tired and crabby at the end of a long run, I think to myself, What would Sister Madonna Buder do? I smile and imagine she would compose a haiku that would keep her running for another mile, or ten. Like Sister Madonna, I use the running to push away my anxiety and allow myself time to think about my problems.

When I am quick to pass judgment on something or someone, I think about Sister Megan and shut my mouth, bite my tongue, and change the subject.

When I see injustice happening around me, I think of Sister Simone, and instead of turning away, I try to understand why it is happening and think about ways I can confront it and then change it.

When I need to face something that makes me uncomfortable or squeamish, I think of Sister Joan facing the world of modern-day slavery and force myself to be just a little bit uncomfortable.

When put into a situation that is unjust, I think about Sister Dianna and stand up for myself, no matter the cost. I received an e-mail from Sister Dianna after I sent her the chapter about her, soon before we went to press.

"For years I have sought to erase the memories of the past and to begin life anew. I suddenly realized that in so doing, I forget those who were with me in the clandestine prison. This is something I refuse to do. They are part of my life and a part of who I am today," she wrote. "Thank you, Jo, for once again reminding me that I have no right to forget the past. By so doing, I become indifferent to this crime against humanity that continues to destroy and shatter the lives of so many people around the world."

Today Sister Dianna is working with a group called Education for Justice to create educational resources that explore the root causes of torture and follow its relation to such issues as poverty, war, food scarcity, economic inequality, and climate change.

She continued: "The spoke I'm driving into the wheel

of injustice is in the form of gently nudging others [myself included] to stop standing on the sidelines and connect the dots amongst the issues that lead to torture, human trafficking, and other human rights violations."

While writing this book I quit smoking. I took up running. I bought a juicer and I meditate every day. I grew up a little, embracing adulthood in a way that living in New York City allows you to postpone almost indefinitely. Is it because of the nuns? Some of it is.

As I was writing this conclusion, I stumbled upon a book called *Simple Abundance: A Daybook of Comfort and Joy* sitting on the coffee table of a yoga studio while I languidly waited for a class to begin. I flipped aimlessly through the pages and landed on the day's words of wisdom for January 5. It began with a quote from a woman named Emily Hancock, the author of *The Girl Within*: "Many women today feel a sadness we cannot name," the quote read. "Though we accomplish much of what we set out to do, we sense that someone is missing in our lives and fruitlessly search 'out there' for the answers. What's often wrong is that we are disconnected from an authentic sense of self."

Without meaning to, this quote summed up something I had been learning from the nuns for twenty-four months.

We live in a culture obsessed with finding happiness in the mundane, with being ecstatic every day of our lives.

Books about this quest for fulfillment become instant best-sellers. Nuns are one of the few groups of people that I can genuinely say are happy more often than they are not. There is so much that nuns can teach us about happiness and living an authentic life. Perhaps it is because they lead a life unburdened by the things that can make us unhappy—relationship struggles, fights with kids, worries over our future . . . But I think it has more to do with how they live. They live very much in the present, embracing each moment. They have good habits. Most of the women I spoke to rise with the sun and get eight hours of sleep each night. They told me they work exercise into their day. They eat right and they pray. For most of the sisters, prayer is a form of meditation that they practice every single day without fail. They've taught me to be still, to be contemplative. Through them I have learned that inviting in moments of silence is as nourishing as remembering to eat the right things.

I don't want to make sweeping generalizations about nuns. I am sure there are plenty of jerk nuns out there, but the ones I met were kind, warm, and generous—so much so that I think a sequel to this book should be *How to Be Happy Like a Nun*, which would (or should) become an instant bestseller.

My biggest regret about the book being finished is that I never got all of the women in one place during the writing process. I can't even imagine what that would have been like. Imagine if Sister Joan and Sister Tesa could have traded ideas about how to help women who have endured a life crisis, be it trafficking or prison, reacclimatize to regular life. Imagine if Sister Simone could give Sister Megan legal advice, or lobbying tips to Sister Nora. I am hoping to find a way in the next year to assemble them all in a single panel somewhere. I told Sister Jeannine about the idea as she handed me a sixth homemade scone in her kitchen.

"It would be like *The View*, but with nuns, so it would be so much better," she said, and clapped her hands with delight.

Exactly.

Like me, many of the nuns are still skeptical about Pope Francis.

Sister Simone told me that during Good Friday, right after Francis was elected pope in 2013, she meditated on the fact that he gave her hope, but that she was terrified that hope would be betrayed. Going into another Easter season for 2014, she told me she still felt the same way.

Speaking to the public radio station WBEZ Chicago on the occasion of the pope's first anniversary in March, Donna Quinn said she hadn't seen very much action on the Church's "women issue."

"I see this nice wonderfulness of words in the media," Donna said. "Why doesn't the media pick up on the fact that the Church is all men? All men are in power." The one hopeful sign, she said jokingly, was the pope's decision to ditch his fancy red shoes.

"If he has taken off those expensive shoes and the garb and walked with the people, he is taking that first wonderful step," she said. "There's a lot more to follow, hopefully."

I e-mailed Donna to tell her I liked her joke.

"Hope the readership gets the comparison of shoes to first step toward working with women globally," she wrote back. "Little by little we will change this Church, Jo . . . Love, Donna."

The new pope has shown that he may be willing to make progress on the Church's woman problem, but even if he is willing, it remains to be seen whether he is able. Changing Church doctrine is a multilayered process that would require changing the hearts and minds of hundreds of male church leaders, many of whom have never been required to have any dealings at all with women, much less strong, powerful, and opinionated women.

We can only hope that somehow "Frank" will end up on Sister Simone's bus or that Sister Maureen will be able to meet with him to give him her version of Women 101.

One thing that stuck with me on every subsequent read-through of this book was the strength of the women in its pages. I keep returning to the idea that both Jeannine Gramick and Bob Nugent were asked to back away from gay ministry. Father Bob abandoned a ministry he had devoted half of his life to. Sister Jeannine stayed. All of these women have stayed their course, despite the Nunquisition, despite an institution they have dedicated their lives to telling them they are wrong. I can't think of a better definition of strength in the face of adversity.

In 2012, Sister Joan Chittister delivered the baccalaureate speech to the graduating class at Stanford University. To the crowd of future doctors, engineers, and founders of fancy technology companies, she said:

> *If you want to really be a leader, you must be a truth-teller. Remember, there will be those among the powerful who try to make you say what you know is clearly not true, because if everyone agrees to believe the lie, the lie can go on forever. The lie that there is nothing we can do about discrimination, nothing we can do about world poverty, nothing we can do about fair trade, nothing we can do to end war, nothing we can do to provide education and health care, housing and food, maternity care, and just wages for everyone in the world. Nothing we can do about women raped, beaten, trafficked, silenced yet, still, now, everywhere. If you want to be a leader, you, too, must refuse to tell the old lies.*

That is the thing about nuns. They stopped believing in the old lies a long time ago and started living out their own truths.

I say it so many times in this book: if nuns ruled the world, so many things would be accomplished. I truly believe this. But I didn't start this book as an attack on the institutional Church and I don't want to end it that way. What I do believe is that the Church does itself a great disservice in keeping nuns out of positions of power. I can't even begin to imagine all of the good a female pope could do in the world, but I hope against hope that one day it becomes a possibility.

Sources

Introduction

"Frequently Requested Church Statistics." Center for Applied Research in the Apostolate (CARA), Georgetown University, n.d., cara.georgetown.edu/caraservices/requestedchurchstats.html.

Gibbs, Nancy. "Pope Francis, The Choice." *Time*, December 11, 2013, poy.time.com/2013/12/11/pope-francis-the-choice.

Chapter 1

Becker, Suzanne. "Interview with Megan Rice, June 22, 2005." Nevada Test Site Oral History Project, University of Nevada, Las Vegas, digital.library.unlv.edu/api/1/objects/nts/1247/bitstream.

Broad, William J. "The Nun Who Broke Into the Nuclear Sanctum." *The New York Times*, August 10, 2012, page A1.

Munger, Frank. "Plowshares Protesters Found Guilty of Injuring National Defense, Damaging Government Property." *Atomic City Underground*, May 8, 2013, blogs. knoxnews.com/munger/2013/05/plowshares-protesters-found-gu.html.

———. "Y-12 Protester Sister Megan Rice: 'The Last Time I Looked at My Watch, It Was a Quarter to Five.'" *Atomic City Underground*, August 25, 2012, knoxblogs. com/atomiccity/2012/08/25/sister_megan_rice_the_last_tim.

Zak, Dan. "The Prophets of Oak Ridge." *The Washington Post*, April 30, 2013, washingtonpost.com/sf/wp-style/2013/09/13/the-prophets-of-oak-ridge.

Chapter 2

Basu, Rekha. "Rekha Basu: 'Nuns on the Bus' Possess Credibility That Few of Us Have." Editorial, *The Des Moines Register*, June 19, 2012, desmoinesregister.com/article/20120619.

Campbell, Sister Simone. *A Nun on the Bus: How All of Us Can Create Hope, Change, and Community*. New York: Harper One, 2014.

"Catholic Sisters' Letter in Support of Healthcare Reform Bill." NETWORK, A National Catholic Justice Lobby, Web, March 17, 2010.

Feeney, Lauren. "Nuns on the Bus Brings Light to Capitol Hill." BillMoyers.com, July 4, 2012, billmoyers.com/2012/07/04/the-nuns-on-the-bus-bring-light-to-capitol-hill.

Nichols, John. "Is the Pope Getting on Board with the Nuns on the Bus?" TheNation.com, September 13, 2013, thenation.com/blog/176277/pope-getting-board-nuns-bus.

Chapter 3

Curran, Charles E. *Catholic Moral Theology in the United States: A History.* Washington, DC: Georgetown University Press, 2008.

Innerst, Carol. "A Nun in Any Clothes Is Still a Nun." *The Philadelphia Bulletin*, August 8, 1971, page 29.

Peddicord, Richard. *Gay & Lesbian Rights: A Question: Sexual Ethics or Social Justice?* Franklin, WI: Sheed & Ward, 1996.

Chapter 4

Buder, Sister Madonna, and Karin Evans. *The Grace to Race: The Wisdom and Inspiration of the 80-Year-Old World Champion Triathlete Known as the Iron Nun.* New York: Simon & Schuster, 2010.

Chapter 5

"Fighting Trafficking." *America,* Podcast, October 28, 2013, americamagazine.org/media/podcasts/fighting-trafficking.

Chapter 6

Roose, Kevin. "Nuns Who Won't Stop Nudging." *The New York Times*, November 11, 2011, page BU1.

Chapter 7

Ortiz, Dianna, and Patricia Davis. *The Blindfold's Eyes: My Journey from Torture to Truth*. Maryknoll, NY: Orbis, 2004.

Smyth, Frank. "The Nun Who Knew Too Much." *The Washington Post*, May 12, 1996.

Chapter 8

Morrow, Carol Ann. "Helping Children of Imprisoned Moms." *St. Anthony Messenger*, May 2008.

Chapter 9

Fiedler, Maureen. "Bad Habits? Two Surprise Vatican Investigations of U.S. Nuns May Be Attempts to Root Out—Gasp!—Feminist Beliefs." *Ms.*, Fall 2009, msmagazine.com/Fall2009/badhabits.asp.

———. *Breaking Through the Stained Glass Ceiling: Women Religious Leaders in Their Own Words*. New York: Seabury, 2010.

———. "New Twists in the Vatican Investigation of American Nuns." *The Huffington Post*, January 14, 2011, huffingtonpost.com/maureen-fiedler/new-twists-in-the-vatican_b_807496.html.

Chapter 10

Brachear, Manya A. "A Nun's Long Battle in the War Over Abortion: Sister Donna Quinn Believes in a Woman's Right to Choose. Now, the Vatican May Weigh in About Her Crusade." *Los Angeles Times*, November 15, 2009, articles.latimes.com/2009/nov/15/news/adna-prochoice-nun15.

——— "Nun Decides to Suspend Activism for Abortion Rights After a Rebuke by Her Order." *The Chicago Tribune*, November 4, 2009, articles.chicagotribune.com/2009-11-04/news/0911030573.

Acknowledgments

There were plenty of people who didn't understand why I would want to write an entire book about Catholic nuns. Thankfully, there were also plenty of people who did.

Thank you to Jane Friedman, Tina Pohlman, Rachel Chou, and Libby Jordan for thinking there was a spark of a book in my obsession with badass nuns.

Thank you to Victor Balta at Current TV and Nikki Waller, Aaron Rutkoff, and Carrie Melago at the *Wall Street Journal* for always being willing to indulge me in just one more story about a nun doing something I thought was interesting.

This is the second time that Megan Hustad has helped me turn a manuscript into something people would actually want to read. Without her, I swear, I wouldn't know where commas go.

ACKNOWLEDGMENTS

Thank you to Rachel Sklar, Glynnis MacNicol, and the ladies of TheLi.st for being so supportive, championing strong women every single day and helping me realize that there truly is a place on everyone's bookshelf for these stories. Without Glynnis, I never would have considered naming this book *Forgive Me, Reverend Mother, for I Have Sinned*. Even though it didn't become the title, it was delightful to think about.

Thank you to all of the women religious who work tirelessly at the margins of society, who never ask for credit or acknowledgment. None of the women in this book approached me, and I had to compel most of them to tell their stories. They are humble and brave. They deserve our thanks and recognition.

And finally, thank you to Lady and the Bear for making it possible for me to work, laugh, live, love, write books, and remain a halfway-sane human being throughout it all.

About the Author

Jo Piazza is the author of the acclaimed *Celebrity, Inc.: How Famous People Make Money* and a novel, *Love Rehab*. She is a regular contributor to the *Wall Street Journal* and her work has appeared in the *New York Times*, *New York* magazine, *Glamour*, *Gotham*, the Daily Beast, and Slate. She has also appeared as a commentator on CNN, Fox News, MSNBC, and NPR.

Piazza holds an undergraduate degree in economics from the University of Pennsylvania, a masters in journalism from Columbia University, and a masters in religious studies from New York University. She lives in New York City with her giant dog.

EBOOKS BY JO PIAZZA

FROM OPEN ROAD MEDIA

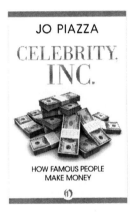

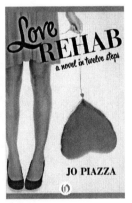

Available wherever ebooks are sold

CPSIA information can be obtained at www.ICGtesting.com
Printed in the USA
BVOW05s2202270814

364614BV00001B/1/P

9 781497 601901